F. BASILE • J. D'ANDRIA URSOLEO • C. MOORE

Edizione 2019
COMPUTER BASED

IN LINEA CON LE
NUOVE INDICAZIONI
INVALSI

PROVE NAZIONALI

Scuola **Secondaria** di **Primo Grado**

Inglese

ELI
PUBLISHING

Indice

Francesca Basile, Jacopo D'Andria Ursoleo, Claire Moore

PROVE NAZIONALI INGLESE

Responsabile editoriale: Beatrice Loreti
Redazione: Leonardo Santarelli
Responsabile di produzione: Francesco Capitano
Progetto grafico e impaginazione: Airone Comunicazione – Enea Ciccarelli
Copertina: Curvilinee
Foto: Shutterstock
Disegni: Gianluca Martini

Via Brecce – Loreto
Tel. 071 750701
info@elilaspigaedizioni.it
www.elilaspigaedizioni.it

Stampato in Italia presso Tecnostampa – Pigini Group Printing Division – Loreto – Trevi
18.83.408.0
ISBN 978-88-468-3829-2

L'opera si propone di preparare gli studenti del triennio della Scuola Secondaria di Primo Grado alla nuova Prova nazionale di Inglese, introdotta a partire dall'anno scolastico 2017/2018 in versione Computer Based (CB).

Si compone di due volumi, uno per i docenti e uno per gli studenti.

Il volume per gli studenti è composto da:

1. una **prima sezione (*La nuova prova INVALSI*) con gli esempi ufficiali** commentati e corredati di strategie per risolverli; questo permetterà allo studente di comprendere ciò che viene richiesto il giorno della prova e di trovare le risposte adeguate.
2. Otto **prove propedeutiche (*Tests*)**, aggiornate in base alle più recenti indicazioni ufficiali provenienti dall'INVALSI, che avvicineranno l'alunno alle diverse tipologie testuali previste, facendo prendere confidenza con i linguaggi e le caratteristiche di ognuna.
3. Due ***Extra Sections*** interamente dedicate alle abilità di *Language in Use* e *Grammar Knowledge*, che verranno introdotte in un prossimo fututo.
4. Una sezione speciale intitolata ***Grammar Reference*** e ***Verb Tables*** che guiderà gli studenti a conoscere e a ripassare gli argomenti di grammatica del triennio presenti nelle prove INVALSI.

Tutte le prove proposte sono state pensate e realizzate a partire da un'attenta analisi degli Esempi Ufficiali di Prove pubblicati nel gennaio 2018 sul sito web dell'INVALSI, nonché da una scrupolosa disamina delle indicazioni operative ufficiali fornite dall'Istituto stesso, nel tentativo di fornire a studenti e insegnanti materiali il più fedele possibile al *format* ufficiale delle Prove, consentendoci di offrire uno strumento di preparazione alla nuova Prova nazionale di Inglese completo e aggiornato.

L'opera è completata inoltre da un CD Audio per il docente che contiene sia i file audio dei brani di lettura proposti in ogni prova di *Reading*, che le tracce necessarie per lo svolgimento degli esercizi dell'abilità di *Listening*.

Al termine di ogni prova, una tabella consente agli alunni di registrare i loro risultati al fine di riconoscere il proprio livello di preparazione e di autovalutarsi.

Infine, per familiarizzare con le prove *computer based*, le prove inserite in questo volume sono disponibili anche sul libro digitale in versione interattiva. Riportiamo a tal proposito le Istruzioni fornite dall'INVALSI per lo svolgimento della prova CB (vedi p. 4)

Il volume per i docenti contiene le griglie di correzione delle varie prove assieme a indicazioni didattiche e ai tapescripts di tutte le attività di *Listening*.

Non ci resta, quindi, che augurare a tutti… buon lavoro!

Gli Autori

F. Basile

J. D'Andria Ursoleo

C. Moore

Istruzioni

tratto da www.invalsi.it

READING COMPREHENSION

La prova di Inglese che stai per svolgere è composta da alcuni testi per la verifica della comprensione di lettura. Le istruzioni prima di ogni domanda ti diranno come rispondere. Leggile dunque con molta attenzione. La prima domanda è sempre un esempio.

Hai a disposizione **quarantacinque minuti** per rispondere a tutte le domande. L'insegnante ti dirà quando cominciare a lavorare. Quando il tempo a disposizione sarà finito la prova si interromperà automaticamente. Durante la prova, puoi costantemente controllare il tempo ancora disponibile nella barra che troverai in alto a destra.

Se finisci prima, puoi cliccare con il mouse sul bottone di fine test . **⏭ Fine test**

In questo caso il sistema ti invierà un messaggio che ti ricorderà che una volta confermata l'uscita dal test non sarà più possibile rientrare.
Puoi quindi confermare e aspettare lo scadere del tempo, oppure rifiutare e controllare le risposte che hai dato e/o completare quelle che hai lasciato in sospeso.

Alcune domande a cui dovrai rispondere hanno quattro possibili risposte, ma una sola è quella giusta. Per rispondere, devi cliccare con il mouse nel tondino accanto alla risposta (una sola) che ritieni giusta, come nell'Esempio 1.

Esempio 1

Q1. Frank is

A ( ) Judith's son.
B ( ) Judith's father.
C (x) Judith's brother.
D ( ) Judith's husband.

Se ti accorgi di aver sbagliato, puoi correggere cliccando con il mouse nel tondino accanto alla risposta che ritieni corretta.

Per rispondere ad alcune domande dovrai scegliere l'alternativa corretta tra TRUE, quando l'affermazione è vera rispetto al testo, FALSE, quando invece è falsa rispetto al testo oppure NOT GIVEN quando non è data nel testo (Esempio 2).

Esempio 2

	True	False	Not given
Q1. He loves cakes.	☐	☒	☐
Q2. He has two cats.	☐	☐	☒
Q3. He lives in London.	☒	☐	☐

In altri casi dovrai digitare tu la risposta che ritieni corretta nell'apposito spazio sotto la domanda come nell'Esempio 3.

Esempio 3

Alcune domande richiedono di ordinare una serie di eventi presentati nel testo seguendo la successione cronologica dei fatti. Per rispondere devi cliccare con il mouse ciascuno di essi inserendoli, nell'ordine che ritieni opportuno, nel riquadro vuoto a destra (Esempio 4).

Esempio 4

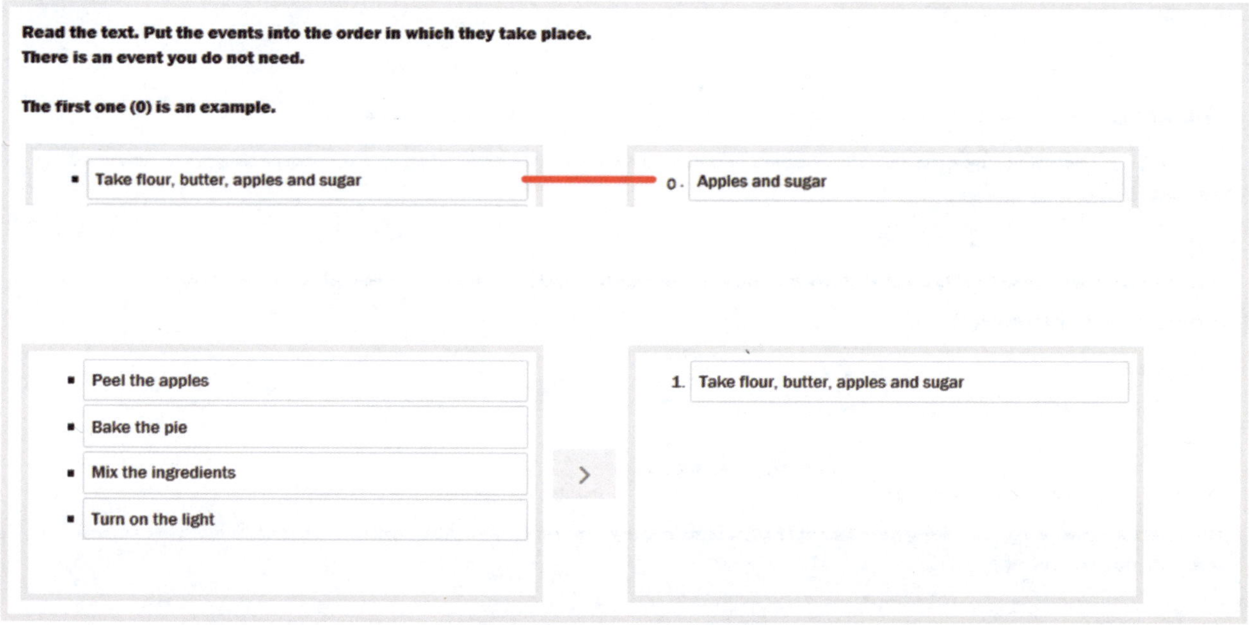

Una volta completato l'inserimento se vuoi modificare l'ordine, in senso crescente o decrescente di uno o più eventi, puoi cliccare su ciascuno di essi e utilizzare le frecce che compaiono accanto alla colonna (Esempio 5):

Esempio 5

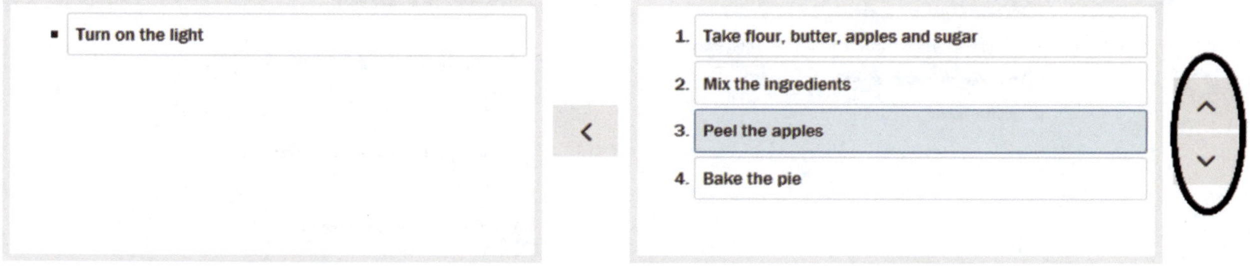

- Turn on the light

1. Take flour, butter, apples and sugar
2. Peel the apples
3. Mix the ingredients
4. Bake the pie

Alcune domande richiedono di inserire in un testo parti mancanti, al posto delle quali è stato messo uno spazio. Per farlo, devi cliccare sulla parte di testo che trovi nella lista disponibile e poi nello spazio corrispondente (Esempio 6). In alternativa, puoi trascinare la parte di testo che ritieni adatta nello spazio corrispondente.

Esempio 6

Read the text about a small hotel in England. Match the missing parts with the gaps (1-3). There is one part you do not need.

The first one (0) is an example.

a private car parking | the perfect place | This 3 star hotel | a quiet setting

Ely Hotel is located in the village of Wolverton 13 miles from Manchester . Guests can enjoy the on-site restaurant.

______ offers you convenience, great value and 18 guestrooms, each decorated in its own style. Ely Hotel is ______ to meet and enjoy fine hospitality and cooking in ______ .

Read the text about a small hotel in England. Match the missing parts with the gaps (1-3). There is one part you do not need.

The first one (0) is an example.

a private car parking | the perfect place | This 3 star hotel | a quiet setting

Ely Hotel is located in the village of Wolverton 13 miles from Manchester . Guests can enjoy the on-site restaurant.

This 3 star hotel offers you convenience, great value and 18 guestrooms, each decorated in its own style. Ely Hotel is the perfect place to meet and enjoy fine hospitality and cooking in a quiet setting .

Alcune domande richiedono di fare degli abbinamenti di diverso tipo scegliendo l'opzione corretta (una sola) tra quelle inserite in un elenco a tendina. Per rispondere devi cliccare nello spazio bianco e scegliere, cliccando l'opzione che ritieni opportuna. L'Esempio 7 illustra uno dei possibili tipi di abbinamento.

Esempio 7

A "I got a smartwatch and new headphones"

B "My parents gave me a new bike"

C "My presents were a pullover, a blouse and new gloves"

D "I received a fantastic camera"

E "I got five books"

Read the expression (A–E) and match them with the sentences (1-3). There is one letter you do not need.

The first one (0) is an example.

0
He can use his present to go to school.
B

Q1. She can use her present to take pictures.
D

Q2. His presents were technological.
A

Q3. She received some clothes.
C

Se ti occorre puoi ingrandire la visualizzazione dello schermo utilizzando i tasti che si trovano in basso alla schermata.

Durante lo svolgimento della prova hai la possibilità di:
a) saltare le domande alle quali preferisci rispondere in un momento successivo;
b) dare una risposta ma riservarti la possibilità di riflettere successivamente sulla risposta che hai dato, prima di terminare il test.

Figura 1

In entrambi i casi puoi cliccare sul pulsante "Segna per la revisione" in basso alla schermata in cui compare ciascuna domanda (Figura 1).

Figura 2

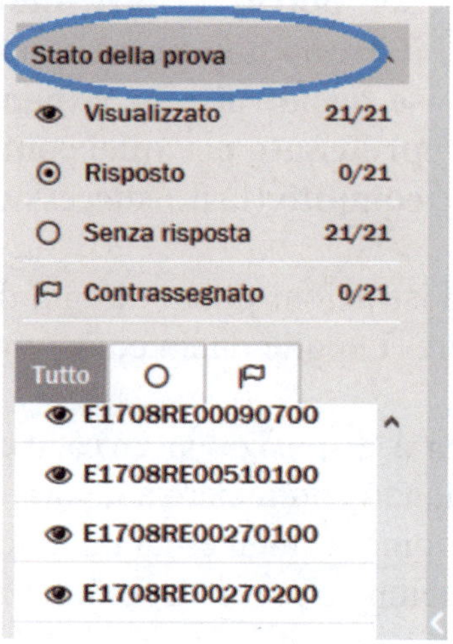

Puoi avere sempre informazioni sullo stato della prova nella barra che trovi a sinistra della schermata. Nella Figura 2 è riportato un esempio.
Con questa barra, in ogni momento puoi conoscere: il numero di domande che hai visualizzato indipendentemente se hai risposto ad esse, il numero di domande a cui hai già risposto, il numero di domande a cui non hai risposto ed il numero di domande che hai contrassegnato per la revisione nei casi a) oppure b) precedentemente descritti come puoi vedere in Figura 2.

Nella barra puoi inoltre controllare, in modo più dettagliato, lo stato di tutte le domande durante la prova cliccando sul tasto "Tutto".

Per avere informazioni limitatamente al numero di domande a cui non hai ancora risposto puoi cliccare sul simbolo.

Infine per tornare solo sulle domande che hai lasciato in sospeso e/o per le quali hai fornito una risposta ma vuoi rifletterci ancora, puoi cliccare sul simbolo .

Se preferisci non visualizzare la barra fin dall'inizio o durante lo svolgimento della prova puoi cliccare sul pulsante Nascondi Revisione.

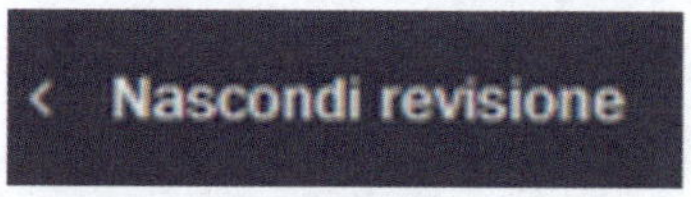

Puoi navigare all'interno della prova utilizzando i bottoni in basso a destra per andare avanti puoi cliccare su , mentre per tornare ad una domanda precedente puoi cliccare su.

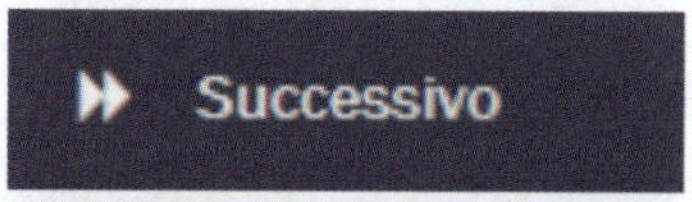

Istruzioni

LISTENING COMPREHENSION

La prova di Inglese che stai per svolgere è composta da alcune domande per la verifica della comprensione di ascolto.
All'inizio di ogni compito (task) una voce leggerà il brano relativo alle domande che vedi e a cui dovrai rispondere.

Ti ricordiamo che:

- **non potrai tornare indietro nell'ascolto del brano.**
- **il brano non potrà essere messo in pausa.**
- **se decidi di non rispondere a una domanda dovrai comunque attendere che il tempo prefissato per quel compito (task) trascorra; solo in quel momento ti verrà presentato il compito (task) successivo.**

Le istruzioni prima di ogni domanda ti presenteranno il compito (task) e ti diranno come rispondere. Leggile dunque con molta attenzione. La prima domanda è sempre un esempio.

Hai a disposizione **circa trenta minuti** per rispondere a tutte le domande. L'insegnante ti dirà quando cominciare a lavorare. Quando il tempo a disposizione sarà finito la prova si interromperà automaticamente. Durante lo svolgimento di ogni compito (task) puoi costantemente controllare il tempo ancora disponibile nella barra che troverai in alto a destra.

Se ti occorre puoi ingrandire la visualizzazione dello schermo utilizzando i tasti che si trovano in basso alla schermata.

Alcune domande a cui dovrai rispondere hanno quattro possibili risposte, ma una sola è quella giusta. Per rispondere, devi cliccare con il mouse nel tondino accanto alla risposta (una sola) che ritieni giusta, come nell'Esempio 1.

Esempio 1

Se ti accorgi di aver sbagliato, puoi correggere cliccando con il mouse nel tondino accanto alla risposta che ritieni corretta.
In alcuni casi dovrai digitare tu la risposta che ritieni corretta nell'apposito spazio sotto la domanda, come nell'Esempio 2.

Esempio 2

Q1. Where is July from?

New York

Q2. What does July have for breakfast?

Milk and cereals

Q3. What is July's favourite subject?

Maths

In altri casi le domande ti chiedono di fare degli abbinamenti. Per rispondere clicca prima sull'oggetto che vuoi inserire e poi sullo spazio in cui lo vuoi posizionare, come nell'Esempio 3. Per modificare la tua risposta procedi nello stesso modo.

Esempio 3

City News

Listen to the city news items. While listening, match the sentence's beginnings (1-5) with the correct endings (A-H). There are two endings that you do not need.

You will hear the recording twice.
You will have 20 seconds at the end of the second recording to complete your answers.
You now have 20 seconds to look at the task.

The first one (0) is an example.

	Headline
A.	Coffee is winner
B.	No more snow today
C.	*Award for finest school*
D.	Everybody wants a holiday – orange juice sold out
E.	Expensive school project started
F.	Write more text messages
G.	Tomorrow's weather
H.	Snow hits city

A B C D E F G H

0. Item 0 C

1. Item 1

2. Item 2

3. Item 3

4. Item 4

5. Item 5

La nuova prova INVALSI

tratto da www.invalsi.it

READING COMPREHENSION

A1 Task 1 | Missing information (one to four words)

Birthday Invitation

Read the invitation card. Answer the questions (1-6). Use a maximum of 4 words. Write your answers in the boxes.

The first one (0) is an example.

Exam Competences

In questo esercizio, trovi un breve testo (in genere un invito, una scheda, un avviso) seguito da alcune domande di comprensione, cui dovrai rispondere usando da una a quattro parole per ciascuna risposta. Per risolvere questo esercizio, segui questi semplici passaggi:

1) Per prima cosa, leggi le domande, per capire quali informazioni cercare nel testo, ed evidenzia le parole chiave.
2) Leggi ora il testo con attenzione e cerca di individuare la frase o il paragrafo in cui si trova la risposta a ciascuna domanda.
3) Se non sai rispondere a una domanda, non preoccuparti! Passa a quella successiva e, solo alla fine, ritorna sulla domanda lasciata in sospeso.
4) Prima di passare all'esercizio successivo, verifica che le risposte fornite siano corrette.

Race over to

Ethan's
Tenth Birthday Party!

Invitation for: *Matthew*

Please come and join in the fun at a pizza sleepover party.

Don' t forget your sleeping bag.

Date: Saturday, August 15
Time: 5:00 pm

Place: 4263 Farmer Road, Salem

☎ 531-553-1324

0 *Who is having a birthday party?*	.... *Ethan* ....
1) How old will the boy be on his birthday?	....
2) Who is the invitation for?	....
3) What kind of birthday party is it?	....
4) When is the party?	....
5) When does the party start?	....
6) Where is the party?	....

A2 Task 2 | Matching opinions to statements

What our visitors think

Read some visitors' opinions (1-5) about York Castle Museum and match them with the sentences (A-G). There is one sentence you do not need. Write your answers in the boxes.

The first one (0) is an example.

Exam Competences

In questo esercizio devi abbinare delle opinioni a delle frasi che ne riassumono il significato. Per risolvere questo esercizio, segui questi semplici passaggi:
1) Per prima cosa, leggi le opinioni riportate.
2) Leggi ora le frasi e, prima di abbinarle alle opinioni, sottolinea le parole chiave.
3) Leggi un'altra volta le opinioni e, per ciascuna di esse, cerca di individuare la frase che ne riassume meglio il significato.
4) Se un abbinamento non ti convince, non preoccuparti! Passa agli abbinamenti successivi e, solo alla fine, ritorna sull'abbinamento lasciato in sospeso.
5) Prima di passare all'esercizio successivo, rileggi gli abbinamenti che hai fatto, assicurandoti che siano corretti.

0	*".... a really interesting trip back in time" A. Lehmann – Bremen, Germany*	*......E......*
1.	".... beautiful city, wonderful museum, great value" Mr & Mrs Ishikawa – California, USA	....
2.	".... the kids really enjoyed the toy collection" Mrs C. Hall – West Yorkshire, England	....
3.	".... best museum we have ever visited, very good value" the Biggin family – Norwich, England	....
4.	".... so much to see, we'll definitely come back" Mr P. Stephens – Gloucester, England	....
5.	".... we didn't want to leave, had a great visit" Z. Howes – Bundoora, Australia	....

A.	They have never seen a better museum.
B.	They enjoyed the museum and the city.
C.	They visited the museum with their children.
D.	They didn't have to pay for their tickets.
E.	*They liked the historical things in the museum.*
F.	They wanted to stay in the museum.
G.	They want to visit the museum again.

A1 Task 3 | Matching sentences to notices

Museum Tickets

Match the tickets (A-E) with the sentences (1-6). You can use a ticket more than once. Write your answers in the boxes.

The first one (0) is an example.

Exam Competences

In questo esercizio, devi abbinare dei brevi messaggi (cartelli, avvisi, post-it, email) a delle frasi che ne riassumono il significato. Per risolvere questo esercizio, segui questi semplici passaggi:

1) Per prima cosa, leggi i messaggi proposti e pensa a dove potresti trovarli: in un negozio? Al bar? Davanti all'ingresso di una scuola? In cucina?
2) Sottolinea le parole chiave di ciascun breve messaggio.
3) Leggi ora le frasi e, prima di abbinarle ai messaggi, sottolinea anche qui le parole chiave.
4) Leggi un'altra volta i brevi messaggi e, per ciascuno di essi, cerca di individuare la frase che ne riassume meglio il significato.
5) Se un abbinamento non ti convince, non preoccuparti! Passa agli abbinamenti successivi e, solo alla fine, ritorna sull'abbinamento lasciato in sospeso.
6) Prima di passare all'esercizio successivo, rileggi gli abbinamenti che hai fatto, assicurandoti che siano corretti.

0	*This ticket was for the 16th October.*	......D......
1)	This ticket was for a child in a group.	....
2)	This ticket cost more than eight pounds.	....
3)	This ticket was for a day in June.	....
4)	This ticket was for the Tower of London.	....
5)	This ticket was for a child and cost nothing.	....
6)	This ticket was for a man or a woman on 15th October.	....

A2 Task 4 | Multiple choice questions

Fun Facts for Kids about Hippos

Read the text about hippos. Choose the correct answer (A, B, C or D) for questions 1-5. Put a cross (☒) in the correct box. Only one answer is correct.

The first one (0) is an example.

Exam Competences

In questo esercizio, devi leggere un testo (come un breve racconto, un articolo di giornale, di una rivista) e rispondere ad alcune domande, scegliendo l'opzione giusta tra quelle proposte. Per risolvere questo esercizio, segui questi semplici passaggi:

1) Per prima cosa, leggi le domande di comprensione proposte, e sottolinea le parole chiave per ciascuna di esse.
2) Leggi ora il testo velocemente, per coglierne il significato generale.
3) Leggi un'altra volta il testo. Questa volta, però, fai una lettura attenta e puntuale, volta a cogliere i punti principali della narrazione, invece del significato generale.
4) Sottolinea le parole chiave del brano e cerca di capire in quale frase o paragrafo sono contenute le risposte alle domande di comprensione.
5) Se hai un dubbio sulla risposta a una domanda, non preoccuparti! Passa alla domanda successiva e, solo alla fine, ritorna sulla domanda lasciata in sospeso.
6) Prima di passare all'esercizio successivo, rileggi le risposte che hai dato, assicurandoti che siano corrette.

Where are hippos born? A hippo baby (called a "calf") is born on land or in water. It is protected by the mother, not only from crocodiles and lions but from hippo bulls that may try to attack them in the water.

What do hippos love? Hippos love water and they spend most of the day in it to stay cool. The hippo can even breathe, see, and hear while its body is under water because its nose, ears, and eyes are on the top of its head.

Do hippos swim better than people? Yes, they are excellent swimmers and can hold their breath for five minutes. Hippos can walk under water along the bottoms of rivers and lakes.

Hungry hippos
Hippos are vegetarians. At night, they come out of the water and feed off the grass.

Are hippos dangerous?
Although hippos are vegetarians, they are still one of the most dangerous animals in the world. Once on land, hippos can run very fast, much faster than people normally can. When a hippo yawns it is not tired but shows its teeth to frighten other animals.

hippo yawning

0. **A calf is**

A. ☐ always born on land.

B. ☐ always born in water.

C. ☒ born on land or in water.

D. ☐ never born on land.

---

1. **The mother protects the calf...**

A. ☐ from hippo bulls.

B. ☐ only from crocodiles.

C. ☐ from other hippo mothers.

D. ☐ only from lions.

---

2. **Hippos stay in the water...**

A. ☐ when they are tired.

B. ☐ to keep themselves warm.

C. ☐ to keep themselves cool.

D. ☐ when they are hungry.

---

3. **A hippo can see and hear when its body is under water because its...**

A. ☐ eyes and ears are under water.

B. ☐ nose is on the top of its head.

C. ☐ nose and ears are under water.

D. ☐ eyes and ears are on the top of its head.

4. Under water a hippo can...

A. ☐ hold its breath for 10 minutes.

B. ☐ move along the bottom.

C. ☐ run very fast.

D. ☐ hear better than on land.

---

5. When a hippo opens its mouth it...

A. ☐ is tired of swimming.

B. ☐ wants to be really friendly.

C. ☐ is bored of eating grass.

D. ☐ wants to scare other animals.

A1 Task 5 | *True/False/Not Given* questions

Read the text about William Shakespeare. Are the sentences 1-7 true, false or not given? Put a cross (X) in the correct box.

The first one (0) is an example.

Exam Competences

In questo esercizio, devi leggere un testo non continuo (quindi associato ad una tabella o ad un grafico) e rispondere ad alcune domande di comprensione a scelta multipla con tre opzioni: ti viene richiesto di decidere se, secondo il testo, le affermazioni sono vere (*True*), false (*False*) oppure non vi sono informazioni sufficienti per rispondere (*Not Given*). Per risolvere questo esercizio, segui questi semplici passaggi:

1) Dopo aver letto le domande che fanno seguito al testo, sottolinea le parole chiave per ciascuna di esse.
2) Leggi velocemente il testo assieme alla relativa tabella o il grafico, per coglierne il senso generale.
3) Leggi ora un'altra volta il testo e la relativa tabella o il grafico. Questa volta, però, fai una lettura attenta e puntuale, volta a cogliere i punti principali della narrazione, invece del significato generale.
4) Sottolinea le parole chiave del brano, e cerca di capire in paragrafo del testo o in quale parte della tabella o del grafico sono contenute le risposte alle domande di comprensione.
5) Se hai un dubbio sulla risposta ad una domanda, non preoccuparti! Passa alla domanda successiva e, solo alla fine, ritorna sulla domanda lasciata in sospeso.
6) Prima di passare all'esercizio successivo, rileggi le risposte che hai dato, assicurandoti che siano corrette.

Will was born in a house which still stands in the small market town of Stratford-upon-Avon. His father John was a glovemaker and his mother, Mary Arden, the daughter of a farmer. Will was the oldest of six (though one of his sisters died when she was only eight).

		True	False	Not given
0	*William Shakespeare was born in London.*	☐	☒	☐
1)	Will had the same name as his grandfather.	☐	☐	☐
2)	Will's father was a farmer.	☐	☐	☐
3)	His mother's name was Mary.	☐	☐	☐
4)	His father, John, had two sisters.	☐	☐	☐
5)	Will was older than his brothers and sisters.	☐	☐	☐
6)	Juliet was one of Will's sisters.	☐	☐	☐
7)	One of Will's sisters died when she was a child.	☐	☐	☐

LISTENING COMPREHENSION

A1 Task 1 | Matching names to pictures

Listen to Miss Elliot describing a picture. Write the people's names in the boxes. The first one (0) is an example.

You will hear the recording twice.
You will have 20 seconds at the end of the second recording to complete your answers.
You now have 20 seconds to look at the task.

Exam Competences

In questo esercizio devi ascoltare la descrizione di un'immagine proposta e scrivere negli appositi spazi i nomi delle persone descritte. Talvolta potresti anche trovare un'immagine con alcuni oggetti e, in questo caso, ti verrà richiesto di scrivere il nome del proprietario di ciascun oggetto nell'apposito spazio. Per risolvere questo esercizio, segui questi semplici passaggi:

1) Per prima cosa, osserva con molta attenzione l'immagine proposta: che cosa rappresenta? Quali sono i tratti distintivi di ciascuna delle persone (o degli oggetti) rappresentati?
2) Durante il primo ascolto, cerca di rispondere a qualche domanda.
3) Se hai un dubbio sul nome da scrivere in uno spazio, non preoccuparti! Passa allo spazio successivo e, solo alla fine, ritorna sullo spazio lasciato in sospeso.
4) Prima di passare all'esercizio successivo, rileggi le risposte che hai dato, assicurandoti che siano corrette.

Miss Elliot's students

Vai al sito www.invalsi.it/areaprove.cineca.it per ascoltare l'audio relativo a questo e agli altri esercizi di *Listening Comprehension*.

A1 Task 2 | Multiple matching with pictures

Children's Jobs

Listen to some children talking about how they get some extra money. While listening, match the pictures (A-H) with the children's names (1-5). Write your answers in the box. There are two pictures that you do not need. The first one (0) is an example.

You will hear the recording twice.
You will have 20 seconds at the end of the second recording to complete your answers.
You now have 20 seconds to look at the task.

Exam Competences

In questo esercizio devi ascoltare alcune persone che parlano di sé e abbinare a ciascuna persona l'elemento giusto tra quelli raffigurati. Per risolvere questo esercizio, segui questi semplici passaggi:

1) Osserva con molta attenzione i disegni o le immagini proposte: che cosa rappresentano? Qual è l'argomento trattato? Fai attenzione: ci sono due immagini in più, che non avrai bisogno di utilizzare.
2) Leggi ora i nomi delle persone nella tabella che fa seguito alle immagini, e presta attenzione all'abbinamento svolto (0) per capire come procedere con gli altri abbinamenti.
3) Durante il primo ascolto, cerca di fare quanti più abbinamenti possibile.
4) Se un abbinamento non ti convince, non preoccuparti! Passa agli abbinamenti successivi e, solo durante il secondo ascolto, ritorna sull'abbinamento lasciato in sospeso.
5) Sfrutta il secondo ascolto per verificare la correttezza degli abbinamenti che hai già fatto e per fare gli abbinamenti mancanti.
6) Prima di passare all'esercizio successivo, rileggi le risposte che hai dato, assicurandoti che siano corrette.

A.

B.

C.

D.

E.

F.

G.

H.

0 John	1. Mary	2. Paul	3. Susan	4. Sarah	5. Lucy
A					

A1 Task 3 | Four-option multiple choice

Pet Discussion

Listen to the conversation between a father and his daughter. While listening, choose the correct answer (A, B, C or D) for questions 1-6. Put a cross (☒) in the correct box. Only one answer is correct. The first one (0) is an example.

You will hear the recording twice.
You will have 20 seconds at the end of the second recording to complete your answers.
You now have 20 seconds to look at the task.

Exam Competences

In questo esercizio devi ascoltare una conversazione fra due persone, in cui si parlerà di argomenti di interesse personale e di eventi tipici della quotidianità e dovrai rispondere ad alcune domande, scegliendo la risposta esatta fra quattro opzioni. Per risolvere questo esercizio, segui questi semplici passaggi:

1) Leggi per prima cosa le domande per capire l'argomento della conversazione, e sottolinea le parole chiave per ciascuna domanda.
2) Durante il primo ascolto, cerca di rispondere a quante più domande possibile.
3) Se la risposta che hai dato a una domanda non ti convince, non preoccuparti! Passa alla domanda successiva e, solo durante il secondo ascolto, ritorna sulla domanda lasciata in sospeso.
4) Sfrutta il secondo ascolto per verificare la correttezza delle risposte alle domande che hai già fornito e per rispondere alle domande mancanti.
5) Prima di passare all'esercizio successivo, rileggi le risposte che hai dato, assicurandoti che siano corrette.

0. **In the morning the girl was...**

A. ☒ at the zoo

B. ☐ in a park

C. ☐ at school

D. ☐ in town

1. **The name of the girl´s friend is...**

A. ☐ Pam

B. ☐ Sam

C. ☐ Ken

D. ☐ Dan

---

2. The girl wants to have a...

A. ☐ horse

B. ☐ dog

C. ☐ budgie

D. ☐ rabbit

---

3. Her friend´s pet has got...

A. ☐ two babies

B. ☐ four babies

C. ☐ six babies

D. ☐ eight babies

---

4. Their house is too...

A. ☐ small

B. ☐ low

C. ☐ high

D. ☐ big

5. One problem with cats is that they...

A. ☐ live too long

B. ☐ eat too much

C. ☐ run after mice

D. ☐ run after dogs

---

6. Hamsters...

A. ☐ are black

B. ☐ climb trees

C. ☐ need a lot of food

D. ☐ live in a cage

A2 Task 4 | Four-option multiple choice with pictures

Plans for the day

Listen to two children talking about their plans for the day. While listening, choose the correct answer (A, B, C or D) for questions 1-5. Put a cross (☒) in the correct box. Only one answer is correct. The first one (0) is an example.

You will hear the recording twice.
You will have 20 seconds at the end of the second recording to complete your answers.
You now have 20 seconds to look at the task.

Exam Competences

In questo esercizio, devi ascoltare cinque brevi dialoghi e rispondere a una domanda per ciascun dialogo, scegliendo l'immagine corretta tra le quattro proposte. Per risolvere questo esercizio, segui questi semplici passaggi:

1) Leggi per prima cosa le domande per capire l'argomento della conversazione, ed osserva con attenzione ciascuna delle quattro immagini proposte.
2) Durante il primo ascolto, cerca di rispondere a quante più domande possibile.
3) Se la risposta che hai dato a una domanda non ti convince, non preoccuparti! Passa alla domanda successiva e, solo durante il secondo ascolto, ritorna sulla domanda lasciata in sospeso.
4) Sfrutta il secondo ascolto per verificare la correttezza delle risposte alle domande che hai già fornito e per rispondere alle domande mancanti.
5) Prima di passare all'esercizio successivo, rileggi le risposte che hai dato, assicurandoti che siano corrette.

0 *Who is answering the phone?*

Toni	***Tim***	**Werner**	**Wendy**
A. ☐	B. ☒	C. ☐	D. ☐

1. Where do they want to go?

	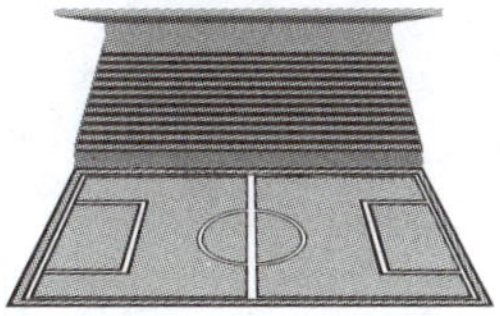		
A. ☐	B. ☐	C. ☐	D. ☐

2. How do they want to get there?

A. ☐	B. ☐	C. ☐	D. ☐

3. When will they meet?

1 pm	**2 pm**	**3 pm**	**4 pm**
A. ☐	B. ☐	C. ☐	D. ☐

4. What will the girl bring with her?

A. ☐	B. ☐	C. ☐	D. ☐

5. What should the girl not forget?

A. ☐	B. ☐	C. ☐	D. ☐

A2 Task 5 | Matching

City News

Listen to the city news items. While listening, choose the headline (A-H) for each news item (1-5). Write your answers in the boxes. There are two headlines that you do not need. The first one (0) is an example.

You will hear the recording twice.
You will have 20 seconds at the end of the second recording to complete your answers.
You now have 20 seconds to look at the task.

Exam Competences

In questo esercizio, devi ascoltare una conversazione più lunga e informale, in cui si parlerà di argomenti di interesse personale e di eventi tipici della quotidianità, e abbinare azioni o oggetti alle persone appropriate. Per risolvere questo esercizio, segui questi semplici passaggi:

1) Leggi per prima cosa i nomi delle persone o cose e degli elementi da abbinare, per capire l'argomento della conversazione. Fai attenzione: ci sono due elementi in più, che non avrai bisogno di utilizzare.
2) Durante il primo ascolto, cerca di fare quanti più abbinamenti possibile.
3) Se un abbinamento non ti convince, non preoccuparti! Passa agli abbinamenti successivi e, solo durante il secondo ascolto, ritorna sull'abbinamento lasciato in sospeso.
4) Sfrutta il secondo ascolto per verificare la correttezza degli abbinamenti che hai già fatto e per fare gli abbinamenti mancanti.
5) Prima di passare all'esercizio successivo, rileggi le risposte che hai dato, assicurandoti che siano corrette.

News item	
0	......*C*......
1.	....
2.	....
3.	....
4.	....
5.	....

Headline	
A.	Coffee is winner
B.	No more snow today
C.	*Award for finest school*
D.	Everybody wants a holiday – orange juice sold out
E.	Expensive school project started
F.	Write more text messages
G.	Tomorrow's weather
H.	Snow hits city

A2 Task 6 | Short open answer

Holidays

Listen to a girl talking about her holidays. While listening answer the questions below. Use a maximum of 4 words. Write your answers in the boxes. The first one (0) is an example.

You will hear the recording twice.
You will have 20 seconds at the end of the second recording to complete your answers.
You now have 20 seconds to look at the task.

Exam Competences

In questo esercizio, devi ascoltare con attenzione un monologo o un dialogo per ricavare le informazioni specifiche necessarie che ti serviranno per rispondere ad alcune domande di comprensione oppure per completare un breve testo con alcuni gaps al suo interno. Dovrai usare da una a quattro parole sia per rispondere a ciascuna domanda che per completare ciascun gap. Per risolvere questo esercizio, segui questi semplici passaggi:

1) Leggi per prima cosa le domande proposte oppure il testo bucato, per capire l'argomento dell'ascolto, e individua cosa ti viene chiesto di preciso.
2) Durante il primo ascolto, cerca di rispondere a qualche domanda oppure di completare quanti più *gaps* possibile.
3) Se non riesci a rispondere a tutte le domande o a completare tutti i *gaps* al primo ascolto, non preoccuparti! Passa alle domande o ai *gaps* successivi e, solo durante il secondo ascolto, ritorna sulle domande o sui *gaps* lasciati in sospeso.
4) Sfrutta il secondo ascolto per verificare la correttezza delle risposte che hai fornito o dei gaps che hai già riempito, e per rispondere alle domande lasciate in sospeso o riempire i *gaps* mancanti.
5) Prima di passare all'esercizio successivo, rileggi le risposte che hai dato, assicurandoti che siano corrette.

0	*When did the girl go on holiday?*	.... *In winter* ....
1)	Who went with her and her parents?	....
2)	How did the family get to Austria?	....
3)	How long did the journey take?	....
4)	What was the weather like? (Give two answers)	a) .... b) ....
5)	What sport did the girl do?	....

Test 1

Section 1 – READING COMPREHENSION

A1 Task 1 | Missing information (one to four words)

Read the following poster for a lost cat. For questions **1-7**, *write the missing information. Use a maximum of 4 words.*

The first one (**0**) *is an example.*

0	*What did the person lose?*	A female cat
1.	What's the cat's name?	....
2.	How old is the cat?	....
3.	Where did the person lose her cat?	In ....
4.	When did the person lose her cat?	On ....
5.	What does the person offer?	A .... £ ....
6.	What's the person's name?	....
7.	What's the person's telephone number?	....

A1 Task 2 | Matching opinions to statements

Read some opinions (**8-12**) *on a famous novel: the Harry Potter books' saga, and match them with the sentences* (**A-G**). *There is one sentence you do not need. Write your answers in the boxes.*

The first one (**0**) *is an example.*

0	*"... very complex plot in the form of a great and entertaining thriller."* *Sally Sunderland – UK*	A
8.	"... very well-written first novel enriched by the author's fantastic imagination" *Sarah Gray – Germany*	G
9.	"... this is a story full of surprises and jokes!" *Dolores Depées – Portugal*	B
10.	"... I would recommend this to anyone who loves fantasy stories!" *Beatrice White – Ireland*	E
11.	"... a really interesting trip back in time thanks to the detailed historical references." *Simon Dubois – France*	D
12.	"... fabulous novel, but the price of the book was quite high." *Francisca Ungaros – Spain*	F

A.	*They found the book's plot very complex.*
B.	They found the book full of surprises and jokes.
C.	They liked the book's location very much.
D.	They think that the book was full of precise historical references.
E.	They found the book suitable for anybody who loves fantasy stories.
F.	They think that the book was a little expensive.
G.	They found the author's imagination fantastic.

A2 Task 3 | Matching sentences to notices

Match the notices (**A-E**) *with the sentences* (**13-18**)*. You can use a notice more than once. Write your answers in the boxes.*

The first one (**0**) *is an example.*

A

CUSTOMER'S NOTE:

Store will not open until 10 am on Thursday because of staff training

B

Mason,
Have a fantastic holiday!
When you get back give me a ring from the airport and I'll come and pick you up.
Dad

C

Library card

You can borrow up to 6 items (books, magazines or DVDs) with your library card.
You can apply for a new card every day from 3 to 5 pm. It's free of charge.

D

From: Fran
To: Colin

I'm having a costume party on Saturday the 5th of February. I know you are travelling home from holiday on that day but come anyway – it doesn't matter when. It won't finish till late.

E

SUPPORT THE ZOO!

TAKE A HALF-DAY GUIDED TOUR TO WATCH OUR ANIMAL KEEPERS AT WORK: £12.00

0	*This notice is for library members.*	C
13.	This notice says that the shop will open later than normal.	E
14.	This notice is from a father to his son.	B
15.	This notice asks for support.	E
16.	This notice contains the maximum number of products a customer can choose.	C
17.	This notice contains the price of a ticket.	E
18.	This notice contains an invitation.	D

A2 Task 4 | Multiple choice questions

Read the following text, then answer questions **19-24**.

COCONUT ISLAND

Coconut Island is the ultimate beautiful, tropical island, rich with coconut palms, golden beaches and clear blue sea. Well, it would be more accurate to say that Coconut Island was a wonderful island. There are fewer coconut palm trees than before because they have been replaced by many tall buildings, hotels, restaurants and swimming pools now. You can still find golden beaches and a clear blue sea, but the sea is full of **speedboats**, noisy jets skis and surfers. All the tourists are happy to spend their holidays on this tropical island: the weather is wonderful, not too hot and quite windy, the food is **tasty** and you don't have to pay a fortune at the restaurant, and the sea is warm all year round. So, why do I feel sad?

First of all, the beach is always crowded with screaming people! There is music from the cafés, there are shouting children, and the hotels are very expensive. The roads look better and there is also a new medical clinic. The local children can speak English and many new businesses are open all the time. The worst aspect of this apparently sparkling island is safety. When an old woman tries to cross the road from her house to the shops, she must be very careful and pay attention. Kids **race** around the island on motorbikes or quads and they don't ride bicycles anymore. I don't know what the world's coming to! Probably this may be called progress?

Glossary

speedboats (n) motoscafi

tasty (a) saporito

to race (v) gareggiare, sfidarsi

19. According to the text:

A. ☐ Coconut Island does not exist any longer.
B. ☒ Coconut Island is a beautiful, tropical island.
C. ☐ Coconut Island has always been full of people, sunbeds and umbrellas.
D. ☐ Coconut Island is not as beautiful as it was in the past.

---

20. According to the text, all of the following are present in Coconut Island but:

A. ☐ clear blue sea.
B. ☐ coconut palms.
C. ☐ hotels.
D. ☒ pineapple trees.

---

21. The writer:

A. ☐ is enjoying a holiday on Coconut Island.
B. ☒ might be the only person annoyed by the new features of Coconut Island.
C. ☐ appreciates all of the new comforts Coconut Island offers.
D. ☐ thinks that nothing on Coconut Island has changed at all.

---

22. Are the following statements **true** or **false**? Tick as appropriate.

		True	False
a	Tourists on holiday on Coconut Island seem happy.	☒	☐
b	Eating on Coconut Island is not as cheap as it should be.	☐	☒
c	The weather on Coconut Island is not always good.	☒	☐

---

23. Today:

A. ☐ Coconut Island's beaches are usually empty.
B. ☒ nothing is as beautiful as it was in the past on Coconut Island.
C. ☐ hotels on Coconut Island are at affordable prices.
D. ☐ his room is in Paradise Hotel.

---

24. In the last paragraph the author:

A. ☐ complains about the noise coming from the children on the beach.
B. ☐ complains about the overcrowded beaches.
C. ☒ states that the island is not as safe as it was in the past.
D. ☐ complains about the absence of new medical clinics.

A2 Task 5 | *True / False / Not Given* questions

Read the following text. Are sentences **25–30** *True, False or Not Given in the text? Put a cross (X) in the correct box.*

What to do after school...

Most schools around the UK have after-school clubs which **are run** by teachers. So let's have a look at one school in Birmingham in central England and the after-school clubs they have on offer…

- One of the most popular after-school clubs at the school is the Art Club: students can do painting and **pottery** and even receive **tuition** from local artists. Every year, the club goes on a trip. Last year the club visited museums and art galleries in London, but this year the club is planning a trip to the Louvre Museum in Paris.

- If you're not very good at Art, then how about volleyball? The school also has a superb Volleyball Club. When the weather is fine, students train outdoors on the volleyball courts but when it rains they play in the school gym. Every month, the team plays in a different **tournament** and wins lots of cups and awards.

- What about joining the Chess Club if you don't like sport? The Chess Club has been active for three years now and students meet in the school library twice a week – on Mondays and Thursdays. Chess is a game which helps improve memory, problem-solving skills, and gives players an **enhanced** ability to think ahead. Chess expert Ivan Lenovic is giving a master-class one evening next term and the Chess Club is very excited!

Glossary

to be run (v) essere gestiti
pottery (n) ceramica
tuition (n) lezione
tournament (n) torneo
to enhance (v) arricchire, migliorare

		True	False	Not given
25.	Most UK schools have Science clubs.	☐	☐	☒
26.	The Art Club visited the Louvre Museum in Paris last year.	☒	☐	☐
27.	The school in Birmingham has a Volleyball Club.	☐	☒	☐
28.	The volleyball courts are bigger than the gym.	☒	☐	☐
29.	The Chess Club started last year.	☐	☐	☒
30.	The Chess Club is only for students who can already play chess.	☐	☒	☐

Fare

Section 2 – LISTENING COMPREHENSION

A1 Task 1 | Matching names to pictures

3 *Listen to Emma describing a picture. Write the people's names in the boxes (**1-5**). The first one (**0**) is an example.*

You will hear the recording twice. You will have 20 seconds at the end of the second recording to complete your answers. You now have 20 seconds to look at the task.

A1 Task 2 | Multiple matching with pictures

Listen to some children talking about the sports they do. While listening, match the pictures (**A-H**) *with the children's names* (**6-10**). *Write your answers in the boxes. There are two pictures that you do not need. The first one* (**0**) *is an example.*

You will hear the recording twice. You will have 20 seconds at the end of the second recording to complete your answers. You now have 20 seconds to look at the task.

A.

B.

C.

D.

E.

F.
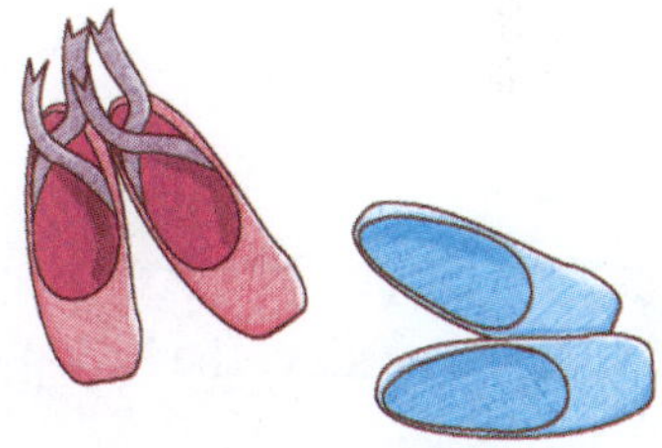

G.
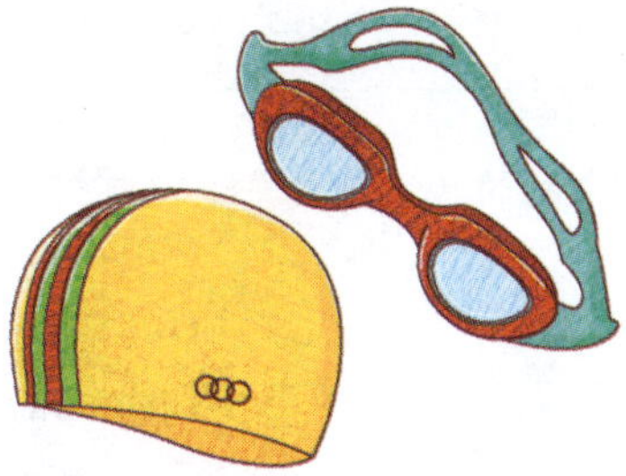

H.

0 *Fred*	6. Jenny	7. Sam	8. Jack	9. Laura	10. Ted
B	....	....	....	....	....

A1 Task 3 | Four-option multiple choice

Listen to the conversation between two friends about a new cinema. While listening, choose the correct answer (**A, B, C** *or* **D**) *for questions* **11-15**. *Put a cross* (X) *in the correct box. Only one answer is correct. The first one* (**0**) *is an example.*

You will hear the recording twice. You will have 20 seconds at the end of the second recording to complete your answers. You now have 20 seconds to look at the task.

Example

0

The cinema is

A. ☐ behind the hospital.
B. ☒ next to the park.
C. ☐ opposite the school.
D. ☐ next to the hospital.

11. The cinema was inaugurated

A. ☐ four weeks ago.
B. ☐ three weeks ago.
C. ☒ two weeks ago.
D. ☐ five weeks ago.

12. The first film the boy saw was

A. ☒ a horror film.
B. ☐ a funny comedy.
C. ☐ a science fiction.
D. ☐ a romantic film.

13. Yesterday, the boy paid

A. ☐ £10.50.
B. ☐ £7.50.
C. ☐ £6.
D. ☒ £8.

14. The speakers are going to the cinema together on

A. ☒ Sunday.
B. ☐ Saturday.
C. ☐ Friday.
D. ☐ Wednesday.

15. On Saturday and Sunday, the cinema opens at

A. ☐ 7 pm.
B. ☒ 7.30 pm.
C. ☐ 8 pm.
D. ☐ 6.30 pm.

A2 Task 4 | Four-option multiple choice

*You will hear five short conversations. There is one question for each conversation. While listening, choose the correct answer (**A**, **B**, **C** or **D**) for questions **16-20**. Put a cross (X) in the correct box. Only one answer is correct. The first one (**0**) is an example.*

You will hear the recording twice. You will have 20 seconds at the end of the second recording to complete your answers. You now have 20 seconds to look at the task.

Example

0 What will the speakers buy Jacqueline?

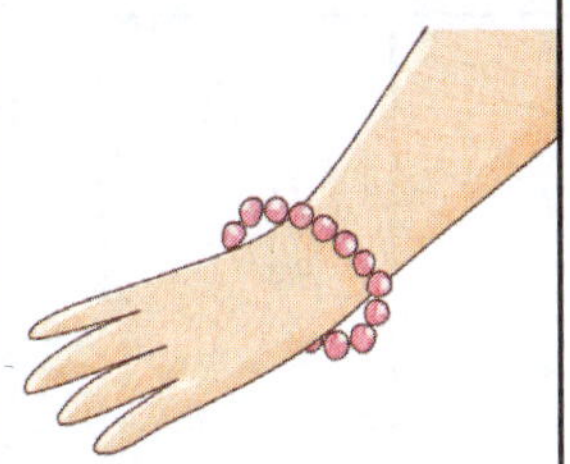			
A. ☐	**B.** ☒	**C.** ☐	**D.** ☐

16. What does the teacher ask the students to bring on the school trip?

			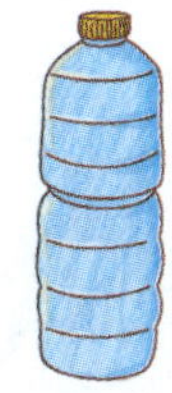
A. ☐	**B.** ☐	**C.** ☐	**D.** ☐

17. What job does the boy want to do in the future?

A. ☐	**B.** ☐	**C.** ☐	**D.** ☐

18. What kind of film does the boy like the most?

A. ☐	**B.** ☒	**C.** ☐	**D.** ☐

19. What time are the speakers meeting at the park?

A. ☐	**B.** ☐	**C.** ☐	**D.** ☐

20. What is the boy planning to do at the weekend?

A. ☐	**B.** ☐	**C.** ☐	**D.** ☐

A2 Task 5 | Matching

Listen to Patrick talking to his cousin Bea about the presents he received for Christmas. What did he receive from each friend? While listening, choose the present (**A-H**) *for each person* (**21-25**). *Write your answers in the boxes. There are two presents that you do not need. The first one* (**0**) *is an example.*

You will hear the recording twice. You will have 20 seconds at the end of the second recording to complete your answers. You now have 20 seconds to look at the task.

Example

0 D Bea

Friends

21. ☐ Mark
22. ☐ Ingrid
23. ☐ Isabel
24. ☐ Kate
25. ☐ Richard

Presents

A. bracelet
B. CD
C. sweets
D. book
E. scarf
F. sunglasses
G. chocolate
H. T-shirt

A2 Task 6 | Gap-fill (monologue or dialogue)

Listen to an advertisement on the radio. Use a maximum of 4 words to complete each sentence (**26-30**). *The first one* (**0**) *is an example.*

You will hear the recording twice. You will have 20 seconds at the end of the second recording to complete your answers. You now have 20 seconds to look at the task.

AUTUMN FEST PARTY!

This fest celebrates the end of (**0**) ....summer........ .

Date: (**26**) .... the 3rd of September.

Time: 10 am - (**27**) .... pm.

Price: £ (**28**) .... per each ticket.

Discounts: free entrance for children under the age of (**29**) .... !

Tickets & Infos: Sunfield Tourist Infopoint, at (**30**) .... Rocky Street.

SELF-EVALUATION

Section 1 - Reading Comprehension		Section 2 - Listening Comprehension	
Task 1 score .../7	Total score .../30	Task 1 score .../5	Total score .../30
Task 2 score .../5		Task 2 score .../5	
Task 3 score .../6		Task 3 score .../5	
Task 4 score .../6		Task 4 score .../5	
Task 5 score .../6		Task 5 score .../5	
		Task 6 score .../5	
		FINAL SCORE .../60	

Ho trovato la prova: ☐ Difficile ☐ Più semplice di quanto pensassi ☐ Adeguata alle mie aspettative e capacità ☐ Altro

Section 1 – READING COMPREHENSION

A1 Task 1 | Missing information (one to four words)

Read the following poster for a trip to the zoo. For questions **1-7**, *write the missing information. Use a maximum of 4 words.*

The first one (**0**) *is an example.*

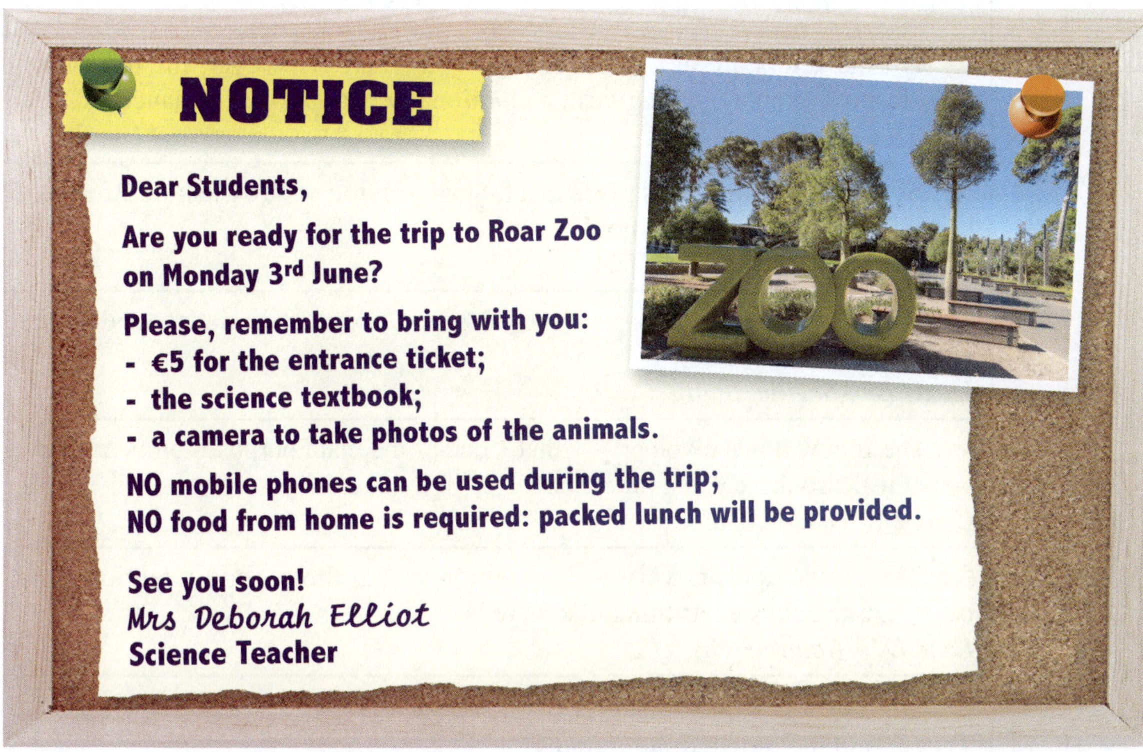

0	*What is the notice about?*	*A school trip*
1.	When is the school trip?	On Monday 3rd June
2.	Where are the students going?	To the
3.	How much does the entrance ticket cost?	€ 5
4.	Which book should the students bring?	The
5.	Why should the students bring a camera?	To take photos
6.	What will the school provide?	packed lunch
7.	What's the teacher's full name?	Mrs Deborah Elliot

A1 Task 2 | Matching opinions to statements

Read some teenagers' opinions (**8-12**) *on a famous film,* Wonder*, and match them with the sentences* (**A-G**)*. There is one sentence you do not need. Write your answers in the boxes.*

The first one (**0**) *is an example.*

0	*"... You will not be disappointed. The violence is normal behaviour which most adults have experienced and is not shocking or brutal, but common in bullying!"* *Benny C. – Bruxelles, Belgium*	F.......
8.	"... All the actors are at the top of their game here. However, the true star is little Jacob Tremblay, who gives an emotionally charged performance." *Cindy D. – New York, USA*	C.......
9.	"... Although the film takes place in a fantasy version of Brownstone Brooklyn, it's more sarcastic than the book." *Rose M. – San Francisco, USA*	G.......
10.	"... It has a wonderful message about tolerance, acceptance, understanding and respect." *Lucas B. – Seville, Spain*	D.......
11.	"... The film will make you cry — that's one of the main purposes of its existence — but it'll also drive you a little crazy." *Colin F. – London, UK*	A.......
12.	"... The movie appears very well intentioned, but those good intentions may be as fabricated as everything else here." *Lane D. – Cohutta, GA, USA*	B.......

A.	They found the movie quite moving.
B.	They found some performances terribly fake.
C.	They really appreciated the actors, especially the protagonist.
D.	They think that the story sends positive messages.
E.	They enjoyed the soundtrack.
F.	*They think that in the film there is some mild violence associated with bullying.*
G.	They compared the film to its book version.

A2 Task 3 | Matching sentences to notices

Match the notices (**A-E**) *with the sentences* (**13-18**). *You can use a notice more than once. Write your answers in the boxes.*

The first one (**0**) *is an example.*

A

B

C

D

E

0	*This notice is for people with dogs.*	D
13.	This notice says that there is a house for sale.	A
14.	This notice says that, in this property, there is a camera.	E
15.	This notice is directed to piano students.	B
16.	This notice was written by a school's headmaster.	B
17.	This notice can be found in a children's play area.	D
18.	This notice regards a rugby match.	C

A2 Task 4 | Multiple choice questions

Read the following text, then answer questions **19-24**.

FLAGS FROM AROUND THE WORLD

During the 2006 World Cup, the English flag could be seen **hanging** from car windows, from the top of houses and in the streets. English flags were everywhere – in fact, during this period, England was just a sea of red and white! Before 1996, however, English people often waved the British flag during football matches, but during the 1996 European Football Championship England played against Scotland and no English football **supporter** wanted to **wave** the 'Union Jack' (the national flag of the United Kingdom), simply because it includes the Scottish flag.

So what do we know about other flags that were flying during the 2006 World Cup? There's the Australian flag, for example, which also includes the Union Jack. The Brazilian flag is written in Portuguese, while the Saudi Arabian flag has religious words written in Arabic. Being written in Arabic, the **flagpole** is on the left of the flag so that the writing can be read from left to right. Another flag flying during the World Cup in 2006 was that of Switzerland, which consists of a red square with a white cross in the centre.

One tricolour flag flying at the 2006 World Cup, however, will never be seen again because, just before the competition, Serbia and Montenegro became independent states. As a consequence, their football team represented a country that simply no longer exists.

Glossary

to hang (v) appendere
supporter (n) tifoso
to wave (v) sventolare
flagpole (n) asta portabandiera

19. During the World Cup in 2006:

A. ☒ many English people started to fly the English flag.
B. ☐ everybody was happy to fly the British flag.
C. ☐ Scottish flags were everywhere.
D. ☐ many English people started to fly the British flag.

---

20. Before 1996:

A. ☒ England played against Scotland.
B. ☐ England was a sea of red and white.
C. ☐ the Union Jack was flying at the World Cup.
D. ☐ people didn't use to fly the English flag.

---

21. Other flags that were flying in the World Cup in 2006 included Saudi Arabia's that has writing on it in:

Arabian ....

---

22. The Saudi Arabian flag:

A. ☐ didn't fly in the World Cup in 2006.
B. ☒ has religious words on it.
C. ☐ has been used on T-shirts.
D. ☐ has a flagpole on the right.

---

23. The Swiss flag:

A. ☐ didn't fly in the World Cup in 2006.
B. ☐ includes a flower.
C. ☐ is square.
D. ☒ includes a white cross on a red background.

---

24. Are the following statements **true** or **false**? Tick as appropriate.

		True	False
a	The Swiss flag isn't a tricolour.	X	
b	The Serbian and Montenegro flag used to be the same.	X	
c	The Australian flag includes the Union Jack.	X	

A2 Task 5 | *True / False / Not Given* questions

Read the following text. Are sentences **25–30** *True, False or Not Given in the text? Put a cross (X) in the correct box.*

The ideal holiday destinations!

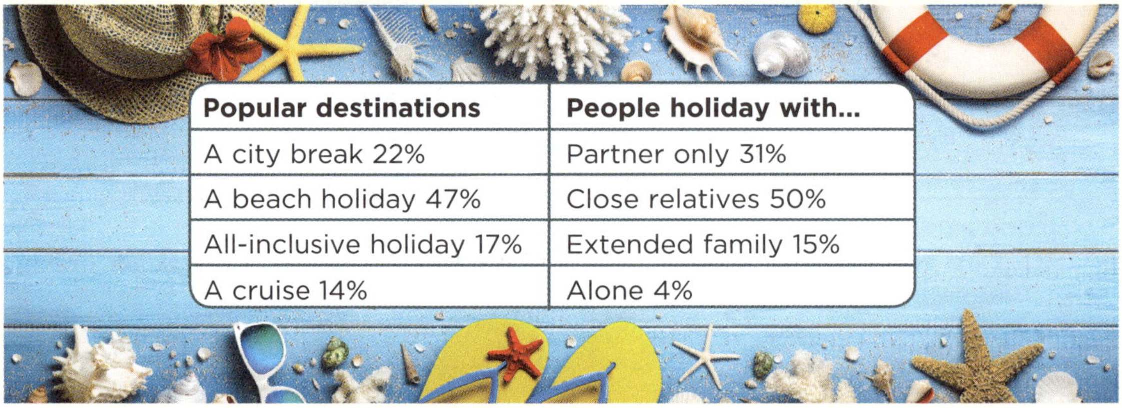

Popular destinations	People holiday with...
A city break 22%	Partner only 31%
A beach holiday 47%	Close relatives 50%
All-inclusive holiday 17%	Extended family 15%
A cruise 14%	Alone 4%

A holiday destination may be the best location for one person but not for another, because it all depends on what you mean by "ideal holiday".

Some places in the world are so incredible that it is almost impossible not to love them. Just think about the millions of people who **queue** at Madame Tussauds Museum to look at the **wax** statues of their favourite singers or actors.

Whichever way you cut it, Mallorca consistently tops all lists for travellers as the most popular holiday destination, thanks to its great beaches, beautiful mountains and various activities suitable for families, couples and even singles. If you want a holiday full of fun and sun, but you can't stand long flights, Mallorca offers the perfect mixture of relaxation and island escape with a flight time of just over 2 hours.

Another favourite holiday destination for young people is the party capital of Europe, Ibiza, which offers fantastic nightlife and lots of opportunities for visitors to enjoy its charming whitewashed villages, sandy coves and pretty pine forests, as well as its legendary club scene.

Most of those who choose Orlando in Florida as their holiday destination, go there to explore its theme parks and to seek fun and sun. However, tourists need to know that there is much more to explore in Orlando besides the world famous Walt Disney, Universal Studios and Harry Potter theme parks. They can also visit interesting museums, beautiful parks, local restaurants and fashion shops. In fact, Orlando represents the most popular destination for British tourists!

Glossary

to queue (v) aspettare in fila
wax (n) cera
whichever way you cut it (v) in qualunque modo la giri

		True	False	Not given
25.	It is most common for people to go on holiday with their partner.	☐	☐	☐
26.	City breaks continue to maintain their leading position as the favourite holiday type.	☐	☐	☐
27.	4% of people prefer to travel on their own.	☐	☐	☐
28.	More than 2 million people visit Madame Tussauds every year.	☐	☐	☐
29.	Mallorca can be very expensive for tourists.	☐	☐	☐
30.	A tourist finds nothing to do in Ibiza.	☐	☐	☐

Section 2 – LISTENING COMPREHENSION

A1 Task 1 | Matching names to pictures

Listen to Lilly describing a picture of her band. For questions **1-5**, *write the musicians' names in the boxes. The first one* (**0**) *is an example.*

You will hear the recording twice. You will have 20 seconds at the end of the second recording to complete your answers. You now have 20 seconds to look at the task.

A1 Task 2 | Multiple matching with pictures

Listen to some women talking about the school subjects they preferred at school. While listening, match the pictures (**A-H**) *with the women's names* (**6-10**). *Write your answers in the boxes. There are two pictures that you do not need. The first one* (**0**) *is an example.*

You will hear the recording twice. You will have 20 seconds at the end of the second recording to complete your answers. You now have 20 seconds to look at the task.

A.

B.

C.

D.

E.

F.

G.

H.

0 *Lizzy*	6. Sveva	7. Beatrice	8. Britney	9. Rebecca	10. Kim
H	A	E	C	G	D

Test 2

A1 Task 3 | Four-option multiple choice

Listen to the conversation between Charlie and his friend Emma about their plans for the weekend. While listening, choose the correct answer (**A**, **B**, **C** or **D**) *for questions* **11-15**. *Put a cross* (X) *in the correct box. Only one answer is correct. The first one* (**0**) *is an example.*

You will hear the recording twice. You will have 20 seconds at the end of the second recording to complete your answers. You now have 20 seconds to look at the task.

Example

0

When would Charlie like to meet Emma?

A. ☒ This weekend.

B. ☐ Tomorrow.

C. ☐ On Monday evening.

D. ☐ Next weekend.

11. Charlie suggests they

A. ☐ go shopping.
B. ☒ play computer games.
C. ☐ go swimming.
D. ☐ go to the beach.

---

12. Emma is going to a concert with

A. ☐ Charlie.
B. ☐ her mother.
C. ☒ her sister.
D. ☐ her brother.

---

13. Charlie's favourite football team is

A. ☒ Manchester United.
B. ☐ Chelsea.
C. ☐ Liverpool.
D. ☐ none of the above.

---

14. Emma is going to the library

A. ☒ on Saturday afternoon.
B. ☐ on Sunday afternoon.
C. ☐ on Friday morning.
D. ☐ on Tuesday afternoon.

---

15. Emma will bring

A. ☐ some sandwiches.
B. ☐ some cake.
C. ☒ some pizza.
D. ☐ some pasta.

A2 Task 4 | Four-option multiple choice

You will hear five short conversations. There is one question for each conversation. While listening, choose the correct answer (**A**, **B**, **C** *or* **D**) *for questions* **16-20**. *Put a cross* (X) *in the correct box. Only one answer is correct. The first one* (**0**) *is an example.*

You will hear the recording twice. You will have 20 seconds at the end of the second recording to complete your answers. You now have 20 seconds to look at the task.

Example

0 What will the speakers buy Jacqueline?

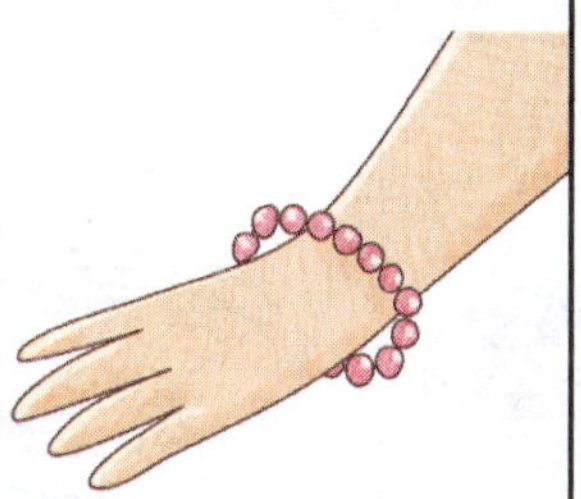			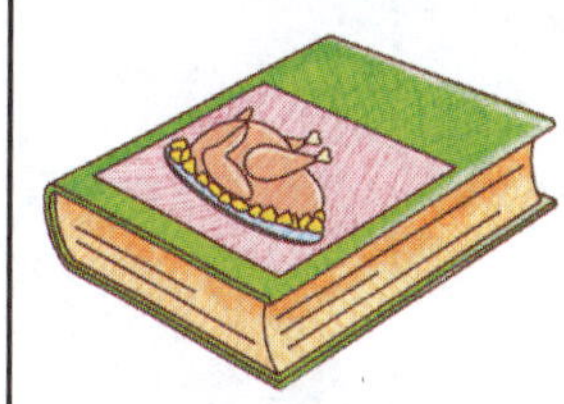
A. ☐	**B.** ☒	**C.** ☐	**D.** ☐

16. Which is the woman's bicycle?

A. ☐	**B.** ☐	**C.** ☐	**D.** ☐

17. How many students went on the school trip?

12	10	8	11
A. ☐	**B.** ☐	**C.** ☐	**D.** ☐

18. How much is the skirt?

A. ☐

B. ☐

C. ☐

D. ☐

19. What will the girl cook?

A. ☐

B. ☐

C. ☐

D. ☐

20. Where is the woman going to go on holiday this year?

A. ☐

B. ☐

C. ☐

D. ☐

A2 Task 5 | Matching

Listen to Lionel talking to a friend about his holiday. What did he do during each day of the week? While listening, choose the day of the week (**A-H**) *for each activity* (**21-25**). *Write your answers in the boxes. There are two activities that you do not need. The first one* (**0**) *is an example.*

You will hear the recording twice. You will have 20 seconds at the end of the second recording to complete your answers. You now have 20 seconds to look at the task.

Example

0 ☐C Monday

Days of the week

21. ☐ Tuesday
22. ☐ Wednesday
23. ☐ Thursday
24. ☐ Friday
25. ☐ Saturday

Activities

A. museums
B. mountains
~~**C.**~~ long walk
D. swimming
E. back home
F. shopping
G. canoeing
H. relax

A2 Task 6 | Gap-fill (monologue or dialogue)

8

Listen to a tour guide giving information on an important museum. Use a maximum of 4 words to complete each sentence (**26-30**). *Write your answers in the boxes. The first one* (**0**) *is an example.*

You will hear the recording twice. You will have 20 seconds at the end of the second recording to complete your answers. You now have 20 seconds to look at the task.

Heriot Museum

YOU CAN SEE:

Downstairs:

– Entrance hall: (**0**) ....old photos..........

– Red room: Italian paintings of important (**26**) ....

Upstairs:

– Right: there are more than (**27**) .... clocks

– Left: there is a collection of (**28**) ....

Price of guidebook: £ (**29**) ....

Museum closes at (**30**) ....

SELF-EVALUATION

Section 1 - Reading Comprehension		Section 2 - Listening Comprehension	
Task 1 score .../7	Total score .../30	Task 1 score .../5	Total score .../30
Task 2 score .../5		Task 2 score .../5	
Task 3 score .../6		Task 3 score .../5	
Task 4 score .../6		Task 4 score .../5	
Task 5 score .../6		Task 5 score .../5	
		Task 6 score .../5	
			FINAL SCORE .../60

Ho trovato la prova: ☐ Difficile ☐ Più semplice di quanto pensassi ☐ Adeguata alle mie aspettative e capacità ☐ Altro

Test 3

Section 1 – READING COMPREHENSION

A1 Task 1 | Missing information (one to four words)

Read the following invitation for a pool party. For questions **1-7***, write the missing information. Use a maximum of 4 words.*

The first one **(0)** *is an example.*

0	*What is the notice about?*	A pool party
1.	When is the pool party?	On Sunday 5th August
2.	Where is the pool party taking place?	At the City's swimming centre
3.	What is the Swimming Centre's address?	....
4.	What time does the pool party start?	At 6.30 pm
5.	What time does the pool party end?	At 11.00 pm
6.	Who is Lola?	She is my sister
7.	What's the sender's full name?	....

A1 Task 2 | Matching opinions to statements

Read some customers' opinions (**8-12**) *about washing machines: match them with the sentences* (**A-G**). *There is one sentence you do not need. Write your answers in the boxes.*

The first one (**0**) *is an example.*

0	*"... My new washing machine destroyed itself while on the spin cycle in the first week and damaged the walls of the laundry room!"* *Isabelle – Maine, USA*	C
8.	"... Front loaders tend to be more energy efficient than top loaders when using warm water, as well as using less detergent." *Paul – Edinburgh, Scotland*	D
9.	"... Top loaders are more energy efficient when washing in cold water and this will help you save money on your bills." *Silvia – Milan, Italy*	....
10.	"... Top loaders are considerably much louder than front loaders. When I switch it on in the evening, it's very noisy and I can't watch TV." *Mark – Dublin, Ireland*	....
11.	"... I purchased my new WM3770HWA washing machine online. Two weeks after my purchase it started having multiple problems." *Susan B.– Nottingham, UK*	....
12.	"... Washing machines have big performance differences in water efficiency, noise, and capacity." *Jaclyn – Ljubljana*	....

A.	The customers would like to have a washing machine which is also a dryer.
B.	The customer bought her washing machine on a website.
C.	*The customer claims that her washing machine broke down after a short time.*
D.	The customer says that washing machines with a front door need less cleaning.
E.	The customer underlines that every washing machine has its own features.
F.	The customer thinks he can spend less on electricity using a top loader machine.
G.	The customer complains about the noise of his washing machine.

A2 Task 3 | Matching sentences to notices

Match the notices (**A-E**) *with the sentences* (**13-18**). *You can use a notice more than once. Write your answers in the boxes.*

The first one (**0**) *is an example.*

A

B

C

D

E

0	*This notice is for people attending Beverly High School.*	C
13.	This notice says that everyone must wear correct shoes on these courts.	B
14.	This notice says that there is a computer for sale.	E
15.	This notice is directed at tennis players.	B
16.	This notice says that there is a special offer for students attending the one-day drama class.	C
17.	This notice says that you don't need to pay to get the bus from here.	A
18.	This notice states that trained service animals are admitted.	D

A2 Task 4 | Multiple choice questions

Read the following text, then answer questions **19-24**.

BRIDGES FROM THE WORLD

Bridges are everywhere, aren't they? They're there to cross a long river, a **crowded** road or a railway line and can be a very exciting experience. If the bridge is particularly high, you may feel like you're flying. If the bridge is very long, it might take you ages to get to the other side. If the bridge is very narrow, you may even be scared of falling off the side!

There are some amazing bridges to **cross** around the world. In the USA, there's the Golden Gate Bridge in San Francisco, in Australia there's the Sydney Harbour Bridge, in Zimbabwe you can cross the Zambezi river to Zambia, while there's the medieval Ponte Vecchio Bridge in Florence and in Thailand the Friendship Bridge to Laos.

Then of course there's London where there are so many bridges. In fact, there are about 214 bridges across the river Thames and 34 of these are in the capital itself. So, the announcement that a new bridge was to be built to celebrate the Millennium was no surprise for many Londoners.

It was to be the first new pedestrian bridge for 100 years with no cars, trains or pollution – just people! Running from St. Paul's Cathedral to Southwark, 320 metres long and 4 metres wide, the Millennium Bridge was opened in June 2000. There was great excitement when the bridge opened. So much so that 100,000 people crossed the bridge in the first weekend; it was a very exciting experience for many, walking slowly across the bridge and looking down at the river 11 metres below.

Glossary

crowded (a) affollato
to cross (v) attraversare

19. The author of the text:

A. ☐ thinks high bridges are very scary.
B. ☐ hates walking across bridges.
C. ☒ suggests you may be afraid on a narrow bridge.
D. ☐ doesn't like bridges at all.

---

20. Zambezi:

A. ☐ is the name of a town in Zimbabwe.
B. ☒ is the name of a river in Zimbabwe.
C. ☐ is the name of a bridge in Zimbabwe.
D. ☐ is the other name of Zambia.

---

21. The Golden Gate is the name of an American:

..........Bridges..........

---

22. In London:

A. ☐ there are exactly 37 bridges.
B. ☐ there are 241 bridges.
C. ☒ there is a large number of bridges.
D. ☐ there are only 30 bridges across the Thames.

---

23. The Millennium Bridge:

A. ☐ is near Chelsea Bridge.
B. ☐ arrives at St Paul's Cathedral.
C. ☐ is accessible to trains and cars.
D. ☒ is 320 m long and 4 m wide.

---

24. In June 2000:

A. ☐ the Millennium Bridge closed.
B. ☐ the author was not so happy.
C. ☐ the author decided not to walk across the bridge.
D. ☒ the Millennium Bridge was inaugurated.

A2 Task 5 | *True / False / Not Given* questions

Read the following text. Are sentences **25–30** *True, False or Not Given in the text? Put a cross (X) in the correct box.*

Wildlife in danger!

Endangered species		
Tiger	Africa/Asia	around 13,000 specimens
Blue whale	world's oceans	fewer than 25,000 specimens
Mountain gorilla	Africa	around 880 specimens
Giant panda	China	fewer than 2,500 specimens

Animals are a beautiful, amazing part of the natural world, and they are also of great global economic importance: they maintain the ecosystems essential to our existence by helping to regulate our climate and by providing clean water, air, food, building and clothing materials and fertile soils.

Even though, there are estimated to be about 30 million animal species on the planet, a large number is in danger of extinction. These endangered species are **threatened** by many things, including habitat loss, **hunting**, disease and climate change. The statistics are quite shocking if we think that current estimates suggest that a third of the world's amphibians, one in eight birds and a quarter of all mammals are endangered.

So, what kind of animals are in danger of extinction? Well, four subspecies of tiger living in parts of Asia – the Caspian, Javan, Balinese, and South China tigers – have already become extinct **due to** habitat loss and hunting by humans. Many are killed for their bones, eyes and skin. Only five subspecies remain.

Then there is the **dwindling** number of whales around the world. Although found in all of the world's oceans apart from the Arctic, there are now fewer than 25,000 living blue whales, the largest animals on the planet. As a result of 20th century whaling, the current population has been reduced by up to 90%, despite the fact that commercial hunting of the species was ultimately banned in 1966.

Glossary

threatened (v) minacciate
hunting (n) caccia
due to (v) a causa di
dwindling (a) in diminuzione

		True	False	Not given
25.	There are more than 25,000 specimens of blue whale in the world's oceans.	☐	☐	☐
26.	Mountain gorillas are moving from Africa to Asia.	☐	☐	☐
27.	Hunting does not represent a cause for animals' extinction.	☐	☐	☐
28.	South China tigers are among the endangered species.	☐	☐	☐
29.	Blue whales live in all of the world's oceans but not in the Arctic Ocean.	☐	☐	☐
30.	Commercial hunting of blue whales has never been banned.	☐	☐	☐

Section 2 – LISTENING COMPREHENSION

A1 Task 1 | Matching names to pictures

*Listen to Patrick describing a picture with different kind of pets. Write the owners' names in the boxes (**1-5**). The first one (**0**) is an example.*

You will hear the recording twice. You will have 20 seconds at the end of the second recording to complete your answers. You now have 20 seconds to look at the task.

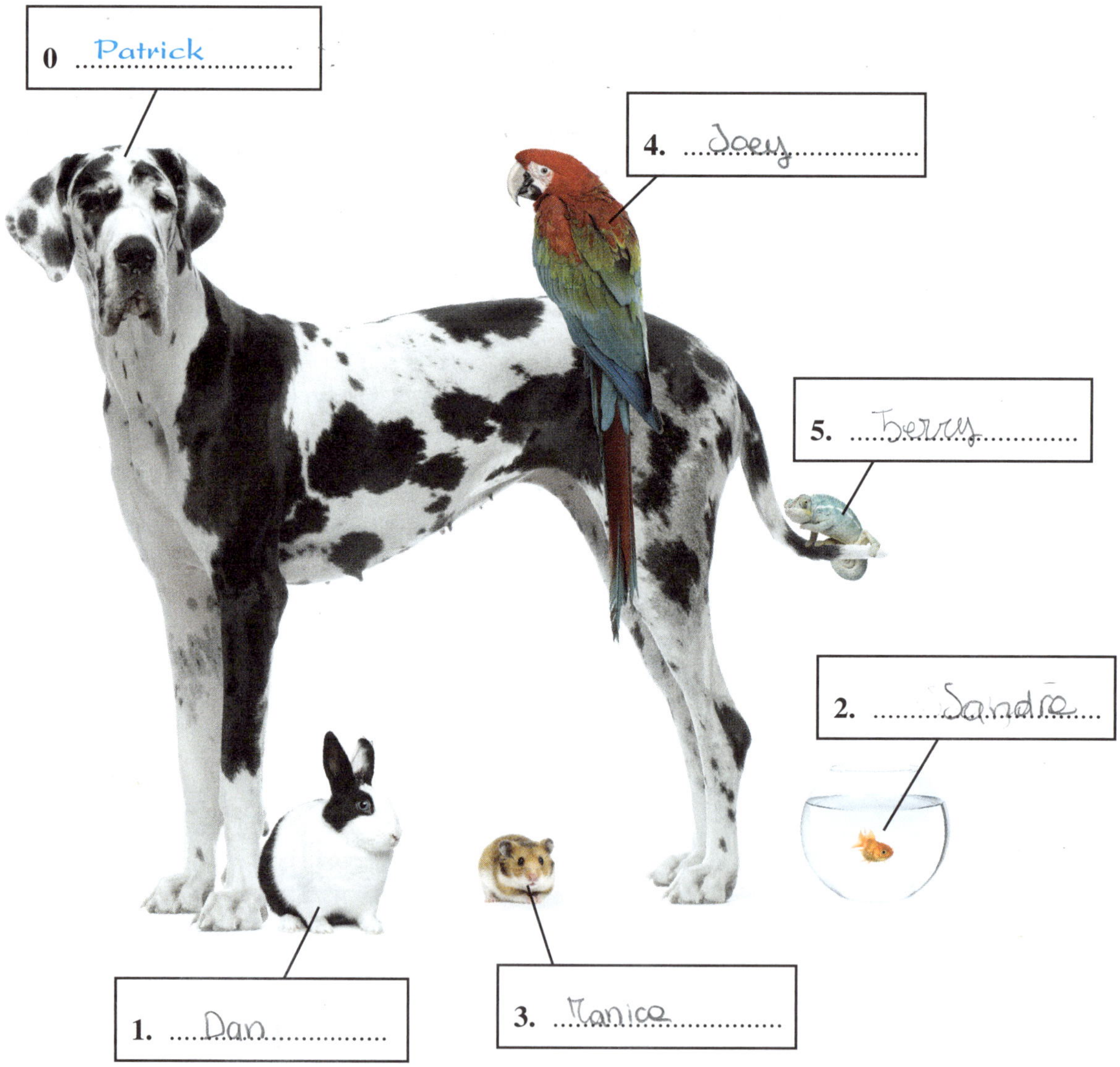

A1 Task 2 | Multiple matching with pictures

Listen to some teenagers talking about their favourite kind of music. While listening, match the pictures (**A-H**) *with the teenagers' names* (**6-10**). *Write your answers in the boxes. There are two pictures that you do not need. The first one* (**0**) *is an example.*

You will hear the recording twice. You will have 20 seconds at the end of the second recording to complete your answers. You now have 20 seconds to look at the task.

A.

B.

C.

D.

E.

F.

G.

H.

0 ***Robert***	**6. Sophia**	**7. Jacob**	**8. William**	**9. Olivia**	**10. Emily**
c	....	....	....	....	....

A1 Task 3 | Four-option multiple choice

Listen to a tour guide talking about the most beautiful places in London. While listening, choose the correct answer (**A**, **B**, **C** *or* **D**) *for questions* **11-15**. *Put a cross* (X) *in the correct box. Only one answer is correct. The first one* (**0**) *is an example.*

You will hear the recording twice. You will have 20 seconds at the end of the second recording to complete your answers. You now have 20 seconds to look at the task.

Example

0

The tour around London will take

A. ☒ three hours.
B. ☐ four hours.
C. ☐ two hours.
D. ☐ five hours.

---

11. At Madame Tussauds Museum you can see

A. ☐ old cars.
B. ☐ statues of famous actors.
C. ☐ a lot of shops.
D. ☐ old books.

---

12. Oxford Street is very famous for

A. ☐ tea rooms.
B. ☐ fashion shops.
C. ☐ exotic restaurants.
D. ☐ coffee shops.

---

13. Big Ben is the nickname for

A. ☐ the Houses of Parliament.
B. ☐ the Great Bell.
C. ☐ the Queen's husband.
D. ☐ the Queen's nickname.

---

14. You can enjoy great views of London from

A. ☐ the Big Ben.
B. ☐ St. Paul's Cathedral.
C. ☐ the London Eye.
D. ☐ the Thames.

---

15. In the summer the Queen goes to

A. ☐ Balmoral Castle.
B. ☐ Buckingham Palace.
C. ☐ the Tower of London.
D. ☐ Windsor Castle.

A2 Task 4 | Four-option multiple choice

You will hear five short conversations. There is one question for each conversation. While listening, choose the correct answer (**A**, **B**, **C** *or* **D**) *for questions* **16-20**. *Put a cross* (X) *in the correct box. Only one answer is correct. The first one* (**0**) *is an example.*

You will hear the recording twice. You will have 20 seconds at the end of the second recording to complete your answers. You now have 20 seconds to look at the task.

Example

0 What will the speakers buy Jacqueline?

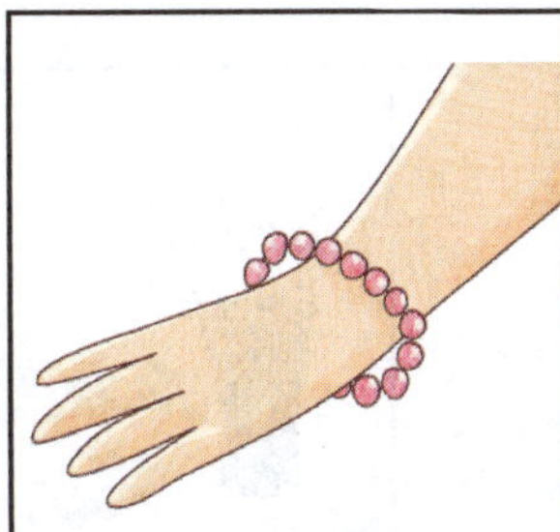			
A. ☐	**B.** ☒	**C.** ☐	**D.** ☐

16. What time was the man's appointment?

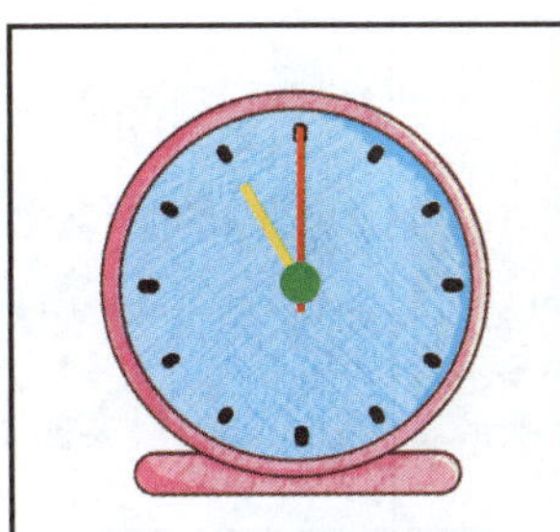		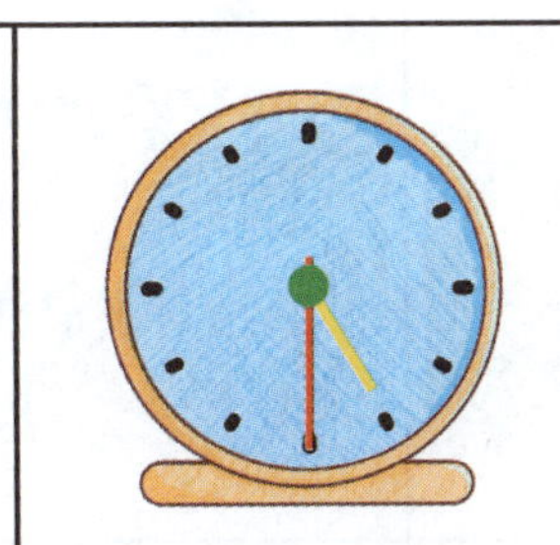	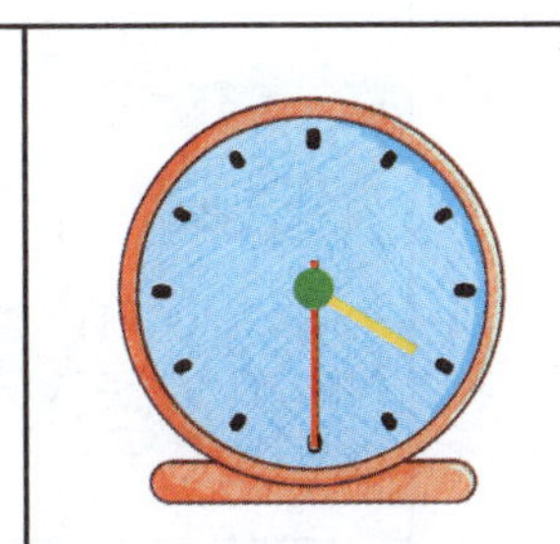
A. ☐	**B.** ☐	**C.** ☐	**D.** ☐

17. What's the weather like in London?

A. ☐	**B.** ☐	**C.** ☐	**D.** ☐

18. What colour T-shirt does the customer buy?

A. ☐	**B.** ☐	**C.** ☐	**D.** ☐

19. What do they decide to order?

A. ☐	**B.** ☐	**C.** ☐	**D.** ☐

20. How far is the best supermarket?

			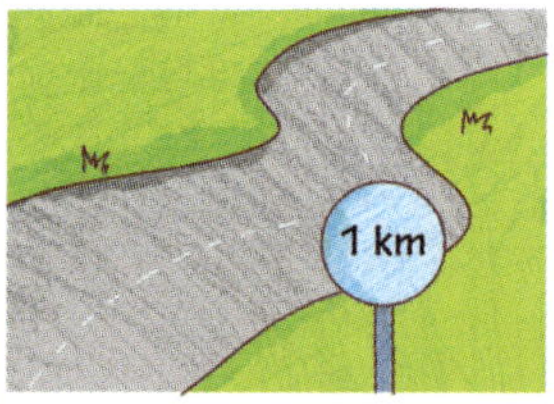
A. ☐	**B.** ☐	**C.** ☐	**D.** ☐

A2 Task 5 | Matching

Listen to a boy talking to a girl about his school teachers. What subject does each professor teach? While listening, choose the subject **(A-H)** *taught by each professor* **(21-25)**. *Write your answers in the boxes. There are two subjects that you do not need. The first one* **(0)** *is an example.*

You will hear the recording twice. You will have 20 seconds at the end of the second recording to complete your answers. You now have 20 seconds to look at the task.

Example

0 ☐H Miss Temple

Teachers

21. ☐ Mrs Davies
22. ☐ Mr Simmons
23. ☐ Mr Brites
24. ☐ Miss Collins
25. ☐ Mr Jones

Subjects

A. Geography
B. French
C. English
D. Maths
E. History
F. Physical education
G. Music
H. Art

A2 Task 6 | Gap-fill (monologue or dialogue)

8 *Listen to a man making a room reservation. Use a maximum of 4 words to complete each sentence* (**26-30**). *The first one* (**0**) *is an example.*

You will hear the recording twice. You will have 20 seconds at the end of the second recording to complete your answers. You now have 20 seconds to look at the task.

Making a reservation

Name of the hotel: Top (**0**) ....Hill.......... Hotel.

The lady wants to book a room for (**26**) the .... weekend of December.

She is staying at the hotel for: (**27**) .... nights.

She books a room with a: (**28**) ....

The room has a view of the (**29**) ....

Her phone number is: (**30**) ....

SELF-EVALUATION

Section 1 - Reading Comprehension		Section 2 - Listening Comprehension	
Task 1 score .../7	Total score .../30	Task 1 score .../5	Total score .../30
Task 2 score .../5		Task 2 score .../5	
Task 3 score .../6		Task 3 score .../5	
Task 4 score .../6		Task 4 score .../5	
Task 5 score .../6		Task 5 score .../5	
		Task 6 score .../5	
		FINAL SCORE .../60	

Ho trovato la prova: ☐ Difficile ☐ Più semplice di quanto pensassi ☐ Adeguata alle mie aspettative e capacità ☐ Altro

Test 4

Section 1 – READING COMPREHENSION

A1 Task 1 | Missing information (one to four words)

Read the following poster for a music festival. For questions **1-7**, *write the missing information. Use a maximum of 4 words.*

The first one (**0**) *is an example.*

0	*Who is the notice directed at?*	*Music lovers*
1.	What is the notice about?	An ....
2.	When is the Music Festival taking place?	On ....
3.	Where is the Music Festival taking place?	At the ....
4.	Where is the English Music Centre?	At ....
5.	What time does the Music Festival end?	At .... pm
6.	Who is the Festival's guest star?	A ....
7.	Who should you contact for further information?	....

A1 Task 2 | Matching opinions to statements

Read some teenagers' opinions (**8-12**) *about mobile phones: match them with the sentences* (**A-G**). *There is one sentence you do not need. Write your answers in the boxes.*

The first one (**0**) *is an example.*

0	*"If you don't have a mobile phone, you also don't have friends. There's a virtual community of people on the Internet and you can't be out of that community and share what you think and do!"* *Gary – Michigan, USA*	A
8.	"I don't think that mobiles are important for our life because they can harm us. They can damage our eyes and ears or give us a memory problem." *Bryan – Montreal, Canada*	....
9.	"Phones have dictionaries, translation apps, timers, calculators, and maps. The Internet can answer any question in less than a minute. The Internet has millions of study resources." *Violette – New Mexico, USA*	....
10.	"Taking a mobile phone with you when you go hiking is a basic safety precaution. If you lose your way or get stuck in bad weather, your mobile phone could just save your life." *Morgan – London, UK*	....
11.	"In the olden days, it could easily take 12 to 14 hours to get to a relative's place. But now even when our relatives are ill we don't bother to visit them. Instead, we just make a phone call." *Brando – Florence, Italy*	....
12.	"With the introduction of Facebook and Instagram, children and teens are on social media and spend most of their time checking their status and 'liking' other people's comments. Social media must be banned for children and teens." *Lowell – Oslo, Norway*	....

A.	*They insinuate that without a mobile phone you are isolated from the world.*
B.	They claim that family values are lost.
C.	They highlight that sophisticated cameras can take professional quality photos.
D.	They think that phones help at school.
E.	They state that teens and children are distracted by social media.
F.	They think that phones can be lifesavers.
G.	They say that mobile phones can cause health problems.

A2 Task 3 | Matching sentences to notices

Match the notices (**A-E**) *with the sentences* (**13-18**). *You can use a notice more than once. Write your answers in the boxes.*

The first one (**0**) *is an example.*

A

B

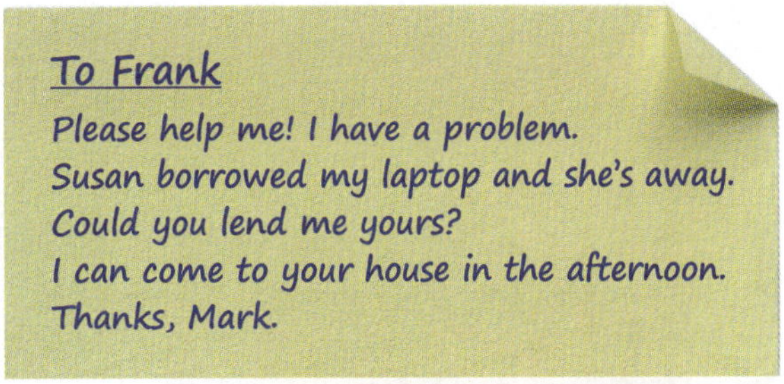

C

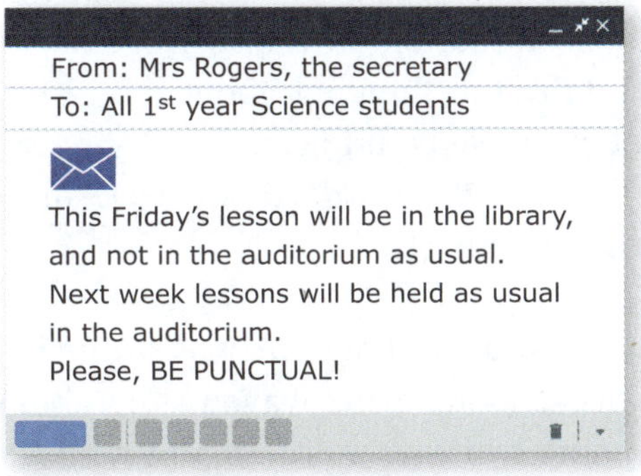

D

E

0	*This notice says that the show doesn't start before 8 pm.*	A
13.	This notice reminds examinees what they are not allowed to do during written exams.	....
14.	This notice can be found in a car park.	....
15.	This notice is from Mark.	....
16.	This notice can be displayed outside of examination rooms.	....
17.	This notice says that the management does not take responsibility for loss or damage of your car.	....
18.	This notice is directed to all 1st year Science students.	....

A2 Task 4 | Multiple choice questions

Read the following text, then answer questions **19-24**.

Love is blind

This is the story of Deshi and a beautiful girl. One day, Deshi was doing his English homework but he was finding it difficult to concentrate on all those irregular verbs he had to learn for the next day. He just couldn't stop thinking about the girl who lived in the building opposite and her beautiful eyes. He could hear her playing some classical music on the piano. It sounded sad. 'She's really good,' thought Deshi, 'but she probably hates it when I play rock music on my guitar!'

The next morning, Deshi saw the girl from the opposite building. She was sitting in her dad's car with the window open. He **dropped** his schoolbag and waved at her, but she just looked at him with her green eyes. That evening while he was doing his homework again, his mum came into the room holding a letter. 'This letter arrived this morning' she said 'but it's for the building opposite. Can you **take it across** while I'm making dinner?' So Deshi left the house and headed to the building opposite. He wasn't feeling very happy.

As he arrived at the building, the door suddenly opened and there she was coming down the steps. At that moment, she dropped something and it bounced down the steps, stopping at Deshi's feet. She said 'Oh hi, I'm Lucy. Are you the boy who plays the guitar?' she asked 'I really like your music.' Deshi couldn't believe what she was saying and when he looked more closely he saw that she was holding a white stick. She was blind.

Glossary

to drop (v) lasciar cadere

to take [it] across (v) portare

19. Deshi:

A. ☐ is a teenage boy from Singapore.
B. ☐ is 15 years old.
C. ☐ is an orphan.
D. ☐ plays the guitar.

---

20. One day, Deshi could not stop thinking about the girl in the building opposite and her beautiful:

....

---

21. Are the following statements **true** or **false**? Tick as appropriate.

		True	False
a	One day, Deshi was doing his English homework.		
b	Lucy plays classical music.		
c	Deshi plays rock music.		

---

22. What did Deshi's mum carry with her one evening?

A. ☐ A letter.
B. ☐ A postcard.
C. ☐ A magazine.
D. ☐ A parcel.

---

23. The term 'waved' (line 8) means:

A. ☐ persist.
B. ☐ gesticulate.
C. ☐ untwist.
D. ☐ straighten.

---

24. Why was the girl holding a white stick?

A. ☐ Because she was blind.
B. ☐ Because she had broken her leg.
C. ☐ Because she had a backache.
D. ☐ Because she was very tired.

A2 Task 5 | *True / False / Not Given* questions

Read the following text. Are sentences **25–30** *True, False or Not Given in the text? Put a cross (X) in the correct box.*

LANGUAGE EVOLUTION

Language is constantly changing and evolving, no more so than the English language which is used around the world. However, when people use English slang, for example, the English language is extended and modified with even more new words and phrases. TV and music also have a big impact on their language, especially as UK singers often sing with American accents without even realising. The English dictionary is also in a constant state of evolution with new words, phrases and expressions being added every year. Young people use a lot of this language, as new words come and go like fashions. Not all slang words or expressions disappear out of the language, however, as sometimes they are so absorbed into the English language that it's no longer pure slang, but a mainstream expression.

British slang dictionary	
Cheers	It can be used as a toast or as a way of saying thank you, or as the signature to emails.
Ace	Excellent or wonderful.
Knackered	Exhausted, tired, also something old or broken.
Scrummy	Something that is delicious.

Words are now also spread by social media, music and TV or video games. A school in Sheffield, in the north of England, for example, recently asked its students to stop using slang words such as *hiya* (hello), *cheers* and *ta* (both mean thank you). It can also be difficult for non-native speakers to understand. However, English language learners perhaps shouldn't worry too much about communicating with native speakers, as research shows that most of the English spoken in the world today is spoken between non-native speakers of the language. But don't give up on slang, as it can be very useful if you watch films or TV in English, read magazines in English, chat online in English or are interested in English song lyrics.

		True	False	Not given
25.	The language young people in the UK use is often very different to that used by adults.	☐	☐	☐
26.	Sometimes British singers don't notice that they sound like Americans.	☐	☐	☐
27.	Teachers have completed a list of modern British slang, which they update every month.	☐	☐	☐
28.	The English dictionary always stays the same.	☐	☐	☐
29.	A head teacher in the north of England thinks using slang can prevent pupils achieving their goals.	☐	☐	☐
30.	Today, most people in the world mainly speak English with people whose mother tongue is English.	☐	☐	☐

Test 4

Section 2 – LISTENING COMPREHENSION

A1 Task 1 | Matching names to pictures

Listen to Ryan describing a picture of the means of transport he and his colleagues use to get to work. For questions **1-5**, *write the colleagues' names in the boxes. The first one* (**0**) *is an example.*

You will hear the recording twice. You will have 20 seconds at the end of the second recording to complete your answers. You now have 20 seconds to look at the task.

0 Ryan

1 ....

2 ....

3 ....

5 ....

4 ....

A1 Task 2 | Multiple matching with pictures

*Listen to some women talking about their dream travel destination. While listening, match the pictures (**A-H**) with the women's names (**6-10**). Write your answers in the boxes. There are two pictures that you do not need. The first one (**0**) is an example.*

You will hear the recording twice. You will have 20 seconds at the end of the second recording to complete your answers. You now have 20 seconds to look at the task.

0 *Elvira*	6. Lorelay	7. Lavinia	8. Zyana	9. Pamela	10. Aysha
E	....	....	....	....	....

A1 Task 3 | Four-option multiple choice

*Listen to two friends talking about a party. While listening, choose the correct answer (**A**, **B**, **C** or **D**) for questions **11-15**. Put a cross (X) in the correct box. Only one answer is correct. The first one (**0**) is an example.*

You will hear the recording twice. You will have 20 seconds at the end of the second recording to complete your answers. You now have 20 seconds to look at the task.

Example

0

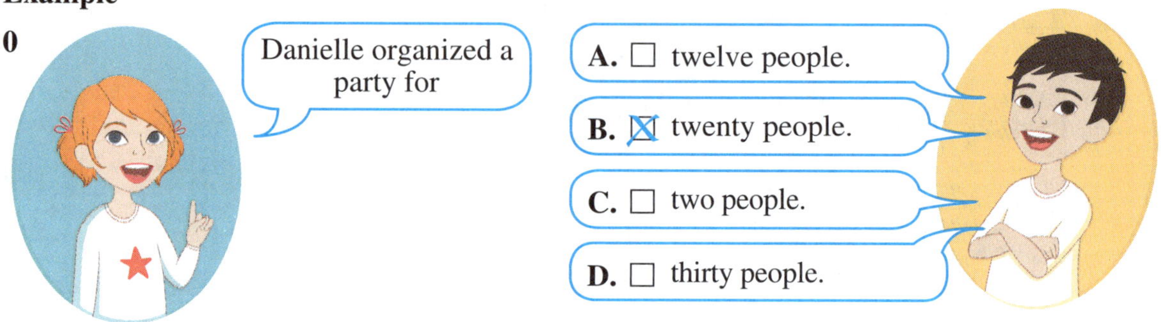

11. She is going to prepare

A. ☐ sandwiches and chocolate cake.
B. ☐ potatoes and cola.
C. ☐ hamburgers.
D. ☐ pasta and pizza.

12. William is going to play

A. ☐ his flute.
B. ☐ Danielle's guitar.
C. ☐ his guitar.
D. ☐ Danielle's flute.

13. Last year her granny made a lovely

A. ☐ scarf.
B. ☐ hat.
C. ☐ shirt.
D. ☐ sweater.

14. Danielle would like to receive

A. ☐ a CD player.
B. ☐ a hoverboard.
C. ☐ a guitar.
D. ☐ a flute.

15. Joey will be at Danielle's place at

A. ☐ 7 am.
B. ☐ 6.30 pm.
C. ☐ 5 pm.
D. ☐ 8 pm.

A2 Task 4 | Four-option multiple choice

You will hear five short conversations. There is one question for each conversation. While listening, choose the correct answer (**A**, **B**, **C** or **D**) *for questions* **16-20**. *Put a cross* (X) *in the correct box. Only one answer is correct. The first one* (**0**) *is an example.*

You will hear the recording twice. You will have 20 seconds at the end of the second recording to complete your answers. You now have 20 seconds to look at the task.

Example

0 What will the speakers buy Jacqueline?

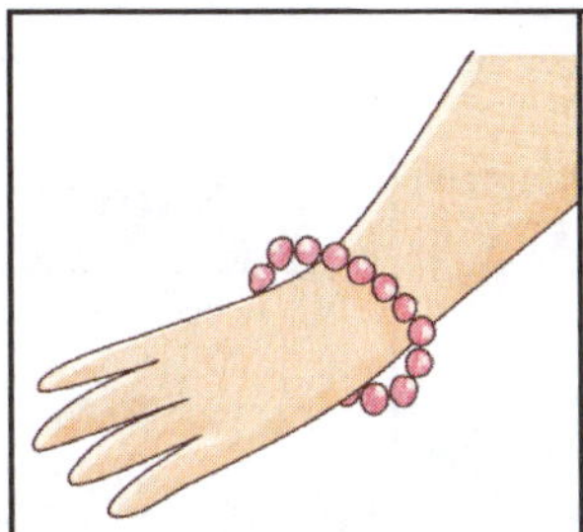			
A. ☐	**B.** ☒	**C.** ☐	**D.** ☐

16. What will Pat do after dinner?

A. ☐	**B.** ☐	**C.** ☐	**D.** ☐

17. What kind of housework does the boy have to do?

A. ☐	**B.** ☐	**C.** ☐	**D.** ☐

18. Where are Thomas and Lily at the moment?

		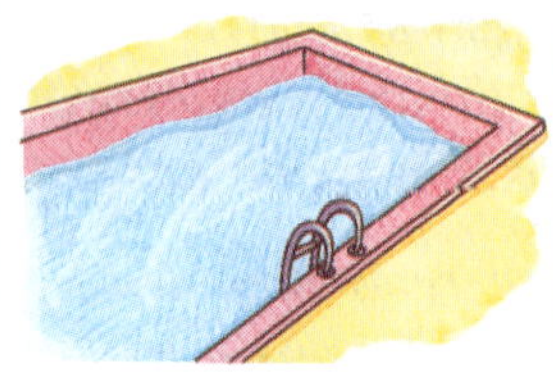	
A. ☐	**B.** ☐	**C.** ☐	**D.** ☐

19. Where do the women decide to meet?

			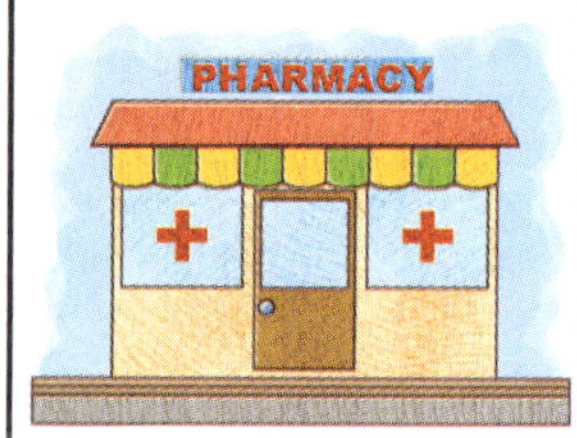
A. ☐	**B.** ☐	**C.** ☐	**D.** ☐

20. What did the friends do on holiday?

A. ☐	**B.** ☐	**C.** ☐	**D.** ☐

A2 Task 5 | Matching

*Listen to a teacher asking her students about their pets. What pet does each student have? While listening, choose the pet (**A-H**) owned by each student (**21-25**). Write your answers in the boxes. There are two animals that you do not need. The first one (**0**) is an example.*

You will hear the recording twice. You will have 20 seconds at the end of the second recording to complete your answers. You now have 20 seconds to look at the task.

Example

0 [F] Teacher

Students

21. ☐ Tom

22. ☐ Marika

23. ☐ Britney

24. ☐ Buddy

25. ☐ Steven

Animals

A. dog

B. hamster

C. rabbit

D. turtle

E. goldfish

F. cat

G. squirrel

H. snake

A2 Task 6 | Gap-fill (monologue or dialogue)

Listen to a presenter talking about a documentary on tigers. Use a maximum of 4 words to complete each sentence (**26-30**). *The first one* (**0**) *is an example.*

You will hear the recording twice. You will have 20 seconds at the end of the second recording to complete your answers. You now have 20 seconds to look at the task.

TIGERS!

The tiger is the largest wild (**0**) ....cat.......... in the world.

A full-grown tiger weighs (**26**) ....

A tiger's tail can be up to (**27**) .... metre long.

Tigers wait until it is (**28**) .... to hunt.

Unlike other cats, tigers enjoy the water and are good (**29**) ....

You can identify a tiger by its (**30**) ....

SELF-EVALUATION

Section 1 - Reading Comprehension		Section 2 - Listening Comprehension	
Task 1 score .../7	Total score .../30	Task 1 score .../5	Total score .../30
Task 2 score .../5		Task 2 score .../5	
Task 3 score .../6		Task 3 score .../5	
Task 4 score .../6		Task 4 score .../5	
Task 5 score .../6		Task 5 score .../5	
		Task 6 score .../5	
		FINAL SCORE .../60	

Ho trovato la prova: ☐ Difficile ☐ Più semplice di quanto pensassi ☐ Adeguata alle mie aspettative e capacità ☐ Altro

Test 5

Section 1 – READING COMPREHENSION

A1 Task 1 | Missing information (one to four words)

Read the following poster for a summer camp. For questions **1-7**, *write the missing information. Use a maximum of 4 words.*

The first one (**0**) *is an example.*

0	*What is the adventure summer camp's name?*	Great Forest
1.	When does the adventure summer camp start?	On ....
2.	When does the adventure summer camp end?	On ....
3.	What is the minimum age required to take part in the adventure summer camp?	....
4.	What will you learn on the adventure summer camp?	You will learn about ....
5.	What will you observe in the adventure summer camp?	You will observe ....
6.	Where is the "Great Forest" adventure summer camp?	At ....
7.	Who should you contact for further information?	....

A1 Task 2 | Matching opinions to statements

Read some people's opinions (**8-12**) *about the Olympic Games: match them with the sentences* (**A-G**). *There is one sentence you do not need. Write your answers in the boxes.*

The first one (**0**) *is an example.*

0	*"...The Olympics also provide jobs since the preparation and the execution of the event requires a large number of staff as well as people with different skills."* *Adrianne – Nice, France*	G.......
8.	"... It is not a waste of money. It gives people something to cheer for and allows them to support their own community. It is a time when everybody comes together." *Jeffrey – Oxford, UK*	....
9.	"...The Olympics celebrate our spirit of competition and the best abilities of each participant. This is a good thing." *Audrey – Cape Town, South Africa*	....
10.	"...The money used for building the facilities of the Olympic games should be given to poor people." *Jackson – Charlotte, USA*	....
11.	"...The Olympic Games bring all nations and different people together to choose champions in various skills and sports." *Rupert – Berlin, Germany*	....
12.	"...The investment in the Olympics is good for the whole economy. Better transport helps to improve tourism and local business." *Maximillian – Cambridge, UK*	....

A.	They say that the Olympics make people feel like a community.
B.	They consider them an opportunity for all nations to interact.
C.	They suggest setting the Olympic Games only in Europe.
D.	They say that the Olympic Games celebrate the best in human beings.
E.	They believe that the Olympics helps tourism and local economies.
F.	They think that money should be used for other reasons.
G.	*They believe that the Olympic Games gives job opportunities.*

A2 Task 3 | Matching sentences to notices

Match the notices (**A-E**) *with the sentences* (**13-18**). *You can use a notice more than once. Write your answers in the boxes.*

The first one (**0**) *is an example.*

A

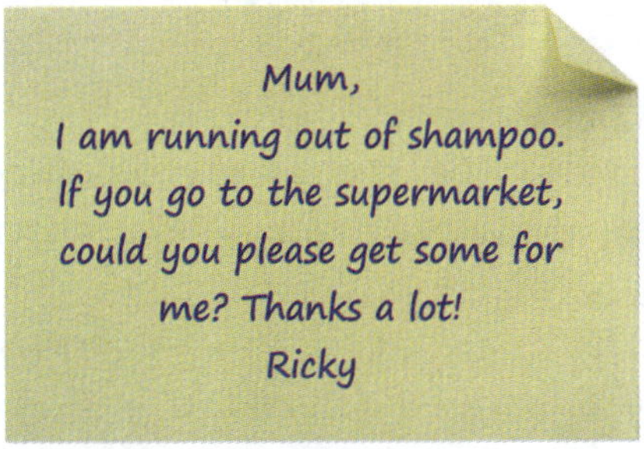

B

C

D

E

0	*This notice says that someone is running out of shampoo.*	A
13.	This notice says that you may find something that you lost.	....
14.	This notice says it is necessary to **go on an errand**.	....
15.	This notice can be found in a zoo.	....
16.	This notice is from Ricky to his mother.	....
17.	This notice reminds you to pick up the kids.	....
18.	This notice can be found in a hotel.	....

Glossary

to go on an errand (v) sbrigare delle commissioni

A2 Task 4 | Multiple choice questions

Read the following text, then answer questions **19-24**.

Cinco de Mayo

Guacamole and fajitas. Mexican flags and mariachi bands. It's May 5th, and America is celebrating *Cinco de Mayo* – but why? This special day is still celebrated in two states of Mexico, but the local **tributes** appear to be unimportant when compared to the giant celebration in the United States, complete with restaurant specials, high-volume advertising and endless promotion. The United States and Mexico have had complex relations for a long time, but the two countries are united in one thing, and that's the celebration called *Cinco de Mayo*.

Cinco de Mayo is Spanish for 'fifth of May.' It **commemorates** the victory of the Mexicans over the French at the Battle of Puebla on May 5th, 1862. The battle was part of the French-Mexican war of 1861 to 1867. The Mexicans won the battle, but lost the war. However, because the French had 2,000 more troops than the Mexicans at Puebla, it was a **source** of enormous pride for them – and still is today! Four days after the battle, on May 9th, 1862, the President of Mexico, Benito Juárez, declared the anniversary of the battle a national holiday.

Today, *Cinco de Mayo* is a holiday in the states of Puebla and Veracruz in Mexico. And since the 1950s, it has been celebrated in many US cities, where it became really popular in the 1980s.

In Mexico, *Cinco de Mayo* continues to be a celebration of the anniversary of the Battle of Puebla. But in the United States, it has evolved into a celebration of Mexican culture and **heritage**. There are hundreds of events around the country. Many of them have traditional Mexican music, dancing and food. And many schools have special events to educate students about the day's historical significance. People sometimes confuse *Cinco de Mayo* with Mexican Independence Day. But that's another celebration, on September 16th.

Felices fiestas!

Glossary

tributes (n) celebrazioni
to commemorate (v) commemorare
source (n) fonte, motivo
heritage (n) patrimonio

19. On May 5th in Mexico:

A. ☐ you can eat guacamole and fajitas.
B. ☐ a festival is celebrated.
C. ☐ you usually go to the restaurant.
D. ☐ you stay at home.

---

20. Even if the United States and Mexico have had complex relations for a long time, the two countries are united by a:

....

---

21. Are the following statements **true** or **false**? Tick as appropriate.

		True	False
a	The Battle of Puebla took place on May 5th, 1862.		
b	The Battle of Puebla was part of the French-Mexican war from 1861 to 1867.		
c	The Mexicans won the war, but lost the Battle of Puebla.		

---

22. The term 'troops' (line 11) means:

A. ☐ soldiers.
B. ☐ multitude.
C. ☐ gang.
D. ☐ company.

---

23. According to the text:

A. ☐ today, *Cinco de Mayo* is a holiday in only two of the states in Mexico.
B. ☐ California was Mexican territory until the 1940s.
C. ☐ since the 1950s, *Cinco de Mayo* has been celebrated in few US cities.
D. ☐ Puebla and Veracruz are two cities in Mexico.

---

24. According to the text, which of the following sentences is correct?

A. ☐ On May 9th, 1862, President Benito Juárez declared the anniversary of the battle a national holiday.
B. ☐ *Cinco de Mayo* is a French festival.
C. ☐ There was a battle in 1876.
D. ☐ *Cinco de Mayo* is not celebrated in the United States.

A2 Task 5 | *True / False / Not Given* questions

Read the following text. Are sentences **25-30** *True, False or Not Given in the text? Put a cross (X) in the correct box.*

GO GREEN!

There is rubbish all over the world and just not enough space to dispose of it. At the very heart of the 'Go Green' global movement are the 3 R's – that is Reduce, Reuse, Recycle. To save our planet, the so-called three Rs are essential in dealing with the waste we produce.

Everyone can contribute. One thing we can all do is start buying things that don't have a lot of packaging or simply borrow things that we don't use very often, instead of buying them. We should also think about our use of electricity. Whenever possible, use natural lighting instead of electric lighting. Try to use fluorescent bulbs rather than incandescent bulbs, and when you use the washing machine, select cooler temperatures for washing clothes. Another way of contributing is to think carefully when you go shopping too: don't use plastic bags. Take a reusable bag with you instead. In addition, materials such as paper, aluminium, glass and plastic can also be recycled.

Glass is relatively easy to recycle, and so too is aluminium. Paper is a little more difficult to continuously recycle because the small fibres in paper eventually become very weak and some high-quality paper is too expensive to recycle. But think about your paper use and don't forget to use the other side of the paper! And finally, of course, we should think about the car we drive. Try to buy a fuel efficient car and don't drive it more than you really need to! Many towns and cities have adopted a car-sharing scheme now and it might be a great idea for getting to work in the morning!

So, as you can see, there are many things we can do in our daily lives to help the environment. Thinking "green" means being aware of and respecting the world around us, and protecting it for future generations.

		True	False	Not given
25.	People all over the world understand that helping the environment is very important.	☐	☐	☐
26.	Incandescent bulbs are more environmentally friendly than fluorescent bulbs.	☐	☐	☐
27.	It's not possible to recycle aluminum over and over again.	☐	☐	☐
28.	There is a limit to how many times paper can be recycled because it is made of small fibres.	☐	☐	☐
29.	It's a good idea to keep the tap on when you're brushing your teeth.	☐	☐	☐
30.	Empty plastic bottles are relatively easy to recycle.	☐	☐	☐

Section 2 – LISTENING COMPREHENSION

A1 Task 1 | Matching names to pictures

Listen to Fran describing a picture of his classroom. For questions **1-5**, *write the classmates' names in the boxes. The first one* (**0**) *is an example.*

You will hear the recording twice. You will have 20 seconds at the end of the second recording to complete your answers. You now have 20 seconds to look at the task.

A1 Task 2 | Multiple matching with pictures

Listen to some people talking about the shoes they prefer to wear. While listening, match the pictures (**A-H**) *with the people's names* (**6-10**). *Write your answers in the boxes. There are two pictures that you do not need. The first one* (**0**) *is an example.*

You will hear the recording twice. You will have 20 seconds at the end of the second recording to complete your answers. You now have 20 seconds to look at the task.

A.

B.

C.

D.

E.

F.

G.

H.

0 *Ella*	6. Adam	7. Jamal	8. Lianne	9. Monica	10. Terence
B	....	....	....	....	....

A1 Task 3 | Four-option multiple choice

Listen to a girl, Rose, talking to a friend about her new classmates. While listening, choose the correct answer (**A**, **B**, **C** *or* **D**) *for questions* **11-15**. *Put a cross* (X) *in the correct box. Only one answer is correct. The first one* (**0**) *is an example.*

You will hear the recording twice. You will have 20 seconds at the end of the second recording to complete your answers. You now have 20 seconds to look at the task.

Example

0

Rose is going to the park

A. ☐ with Jack and Richard.
B. ☐ with Jack only.
C. ☒ with her new classmates.
D. ☐ with Richard only.

11. Richard is going to

A. ☐ the shopping mall with Jack.
B. ☐ the shopping mall with Jack and his brother.
C. ☐ the beach with Rachel and Manuel.
D. ☐ the shopping mall with Rachel.

12. Mary, Rosaleen and Wendy are

A. ☐ Rose's cousins.
B. ☐ Rose's new classmates.
C. ☐ Richard's old friends.
D. ☐ Rose's old friends.

13. The young, tall girl with short curly hair is

A. ☐ Wendy.
B. ☐ Rosaleen.
C. ☐ Mary.
D. ☐ Sarah.

14. Mary is the girl

A. ☐ with long dark hair and blue eyes.
B. ☐ with long dark hair and green eyes.
C. ☐ with short blonde hair and brown eyes.
D. ☐ with short dark hair and blue eyes.

15. Rosaleen is

A. ☐ very patient and hardworking.
B. ☐ very fashionable but unfriendly.
C. ☐ very fashionable and patient.
D. ☐ very friendly and fashionable.

A2 Task 4 | Four-option multiple choice

You will hear five short conversations. There is one question for each conversation. While listening, choose the correct answer (**A**, **B**, **C** *or* **D**) *for questions* **16-20**. *Put a cross* (X) *in the correct box. Only one answer is correct. The first one* (**0**) *is an example.*

You will hear the recording twice. You will have 20 seconds at the end of the second recording to complete your answers. You now have 20 seconds to look at the task.

Example

0 What will the speakers buy Jacqueline?

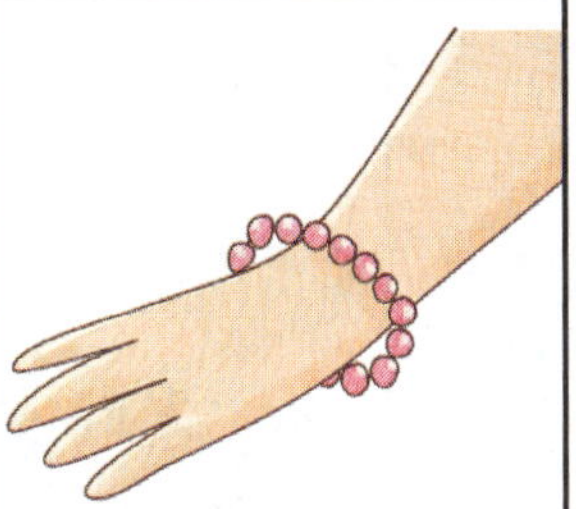			
A. ☐	**B.** ☒	**C.** ☐	**D.** ☐

16. Which is Elizabeth?

A. ☐	**B.** ☐	**C.** ☐	**D.** ☐

17. What does the woman want to buy?

A. ☐	**B.** ☐	**C.** ☐	**D.** ☐

18. What was the weather like at the lake?

A. ☐	**B.** ☐	**C.** ☐	**D.** ☐

19. Where do they stop?

A. ☐	**B.** ☐	**C.** ☐	**D.** ☐

20. How did Ian's family travel to Nice?

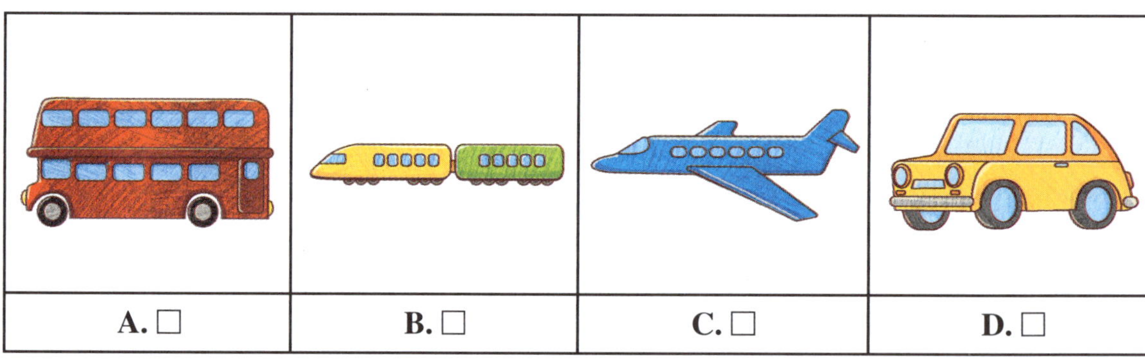

A. ☐	**B.** ☐	**C.** ☐	**D.** ☐

A2 Task 5 | Matching

Listen to Mike talking to his friend Ann about his family members' jobs. What does each member do? While listening, choose the profession (**A-H**) *for each family member* (**21-25**). *Write your answers in the boxes. There are two professions that you do not need. The first one* (**0**) *is an example.*

You will hear the recording twice. You will have 20 seconds at the end of the second recording to complete your answers. You now have 20 seconds to look at the task.

Example

0 ☐ F Cousin

Students

21. ☐ mum

22. ☐ dad

23. ☐ sister

24. ☐ aunt

25. ☐ uncle

Professions

A. doctor

B. actress

C. lawyer

D. pilot

E. teacher

F. nurse

G. tennis player

H. singer

A2 Task 6 | Gap-fill (monologue or dialogue)

8 *Listen to a presenter talking about a local festival. Use a maximum of 4 words to complete each sentence* (**26-30**). *The first one* (**0**) *is an example.*

You will hear the recording twice. You will have 20 seconds at the end of the second recording to complete your answers. You now have 20 seconds to look at the task.

Pizza party!

Date: Sunday (**0**) ....14th........... of June.

When? From 6 pm on Sunday to (**26**) ....

Tickets: £ (**27**) .... per person.

Special discount price: children under the age of (**28**) .... go in for £2!

Contact person: Tracey (**29**) ....

Phone: call Tracey on (**30**) .... to book tickets!

SELF-EVALUATION

Section 1 – Reading Comprehension		Section 2 – Listening Comprehension	
Task 1 score .../7	Total score .../30	Task 1 score .../5	Total score .../30
Task 2 score .../5		Task 2 score .../5	
Task 3 score .../6		Task 3 score .../5	
Task 4 score .../6		Task 4 score .../5	
Task 5 score .../6		Task 5 score .../5	
		Task 6 score .../5	
		FINAL SCORE .../60	

Ho trovato la prova: ☐ Difficile ☐ Più semplice di quanto pensassi ☐ Adeguata alle mie aspettative e capacità ☐ Altro

Test 6

Section 1 – READING COMPREHENSION

A1 Task 1 | Missing information (one to four words)

Read the following party invitation. For questions **1-7**, *write the missing information. Use a maximum of 4 words.*

The first one (**0**) *is an example.*

0	*What is the notice about?*	An ...engagement party...
1.	Who is celebrating their engagement?	.... and ....
2.	When is the engagement party?	On ....
3.	Where is the party taking place?	At the ....
4.	What time does the party start?	At ....
5.	What time does the party end?	At ....
6.	What is the Grand Hyatt Hotel's address?	....
7.	What's Jane's phone number?	....

A1 Task 2 | Matching opinions to statements

Read some teenagers' opinions (**8-12**) *about fashion: match them with the sentences* (**A-G**). *There is one sentence you do not need. Write your answers in the boxes.*

The first one (**0**) *is an example.*

0	*"... When you meet someone, the first thing they learn about you is what you look like. Fashion is a fantastic way to express your personality and let people know who you are!"* *Josephine – Bruges, Belgium*	F.......
8.	"... People who think fashion is important usually have something to prove, hide or say... I believe modesty is better than any other fashion..." *Lionel – Santa Barbara, USA*	....
9.	"...You just need to wear suitable clothes in some situations, for example: you have to wear a uniform to school but you shouldn't wear a suit to a party or a swimming costume to work." *Rose – San Francisco, USA*	....
10.	"... There are too many views of what good and bad fashion is for it to really be anything important. Many so-called fashionable clothes look ridiculous and aren't things any normal person would ever wear." *Sophia – Prague, Czech Republic*	....
11.	"... Most people, especially teenagers, get caught up in fashion from their peers. They want to be part of something and they do it through the newest fashion trends, so that they can be 'cool'." *Oliver – Cardiff, UK*	....
12.	"... Through clothes we can show our personality, what we like and what we don't like. Fashion styles are all a type of art. Fashion keeps us creative, entertains and even gives us confidence." *Merkel – Stuttgart, Germany*	....

A.	They believe people live their lives like a fashion show all the time.
B.	They find creativity in fashion is an important issue.
C.	They suggest that with fashion comes peer pressure.
D.	They think that you have to dress according to the occasion.
E.	They enjoy wearing tracksuits and trainers all day.
F.	*They say that first impressions matter!*
G.	They compare different ways of dressing.

A2 Task 3 | Matching sentences to notices

Match the notices (**A-E**) *with the sentences* (**13-18**). *You can use a notice more than once. Write your answers in the boxes.*

The first one (**0**) *is an example.*

A

B

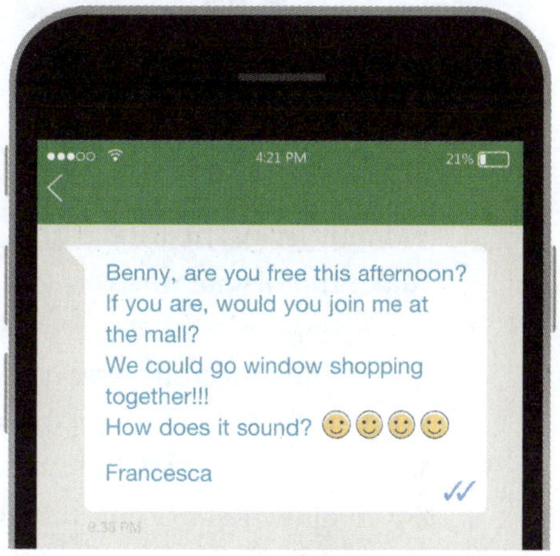

C

D

E

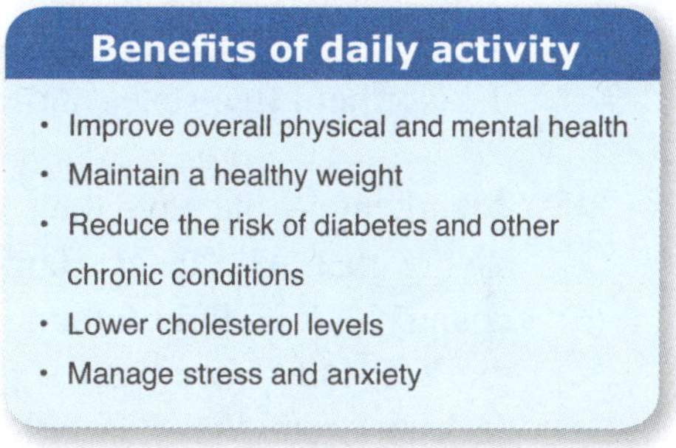

0	*This notice can be found at the airport.*	C
13.	This notice says that only a restricted number of people have access to this area.	....
14.	This notice says to use the stairs instead of the lift in the event of fire.	....
15.	This notice contains an invitation.	....
16.	This notice asks passengers to pay attention to their luggage.	....
17.	This notice is from Francesca to Benny.	....
18.	This notice contains the benefits of daily activity.	....

A2 Task 4 | Multiple choice questions

Read the following text, then answer questions **19-24**.

The woman on the $20 bill

The American Civil War took place in the United States from 1861 to 1865 and aimed to end slavery throughout the country. Both before and during this war, Abolitionism was a movement to end the Atlantic slave trade and set slaves free. In this period, one woman made history – the anti-slavery activist Harriet Tubman, and she is about to make history again.

Having also fought for women's right to vote, she will be the first woman and the first African American to appear on a major US currency note. The front of the new $20 bill will **feature** Harriet Tubman, as she replaces Andrew Jackson, the seventh US President and a slaveholder. His image, instead, will be on the back of the redesigned $20 note. Born in 1822, Harriet Tubman escaped slavery and helped to free others. After having escaped from slavery, Tubman often returned to the South to aid in leading other slaves to safety in the Northern free states and to Canada.

American people gave their views, with many saying that Alexander Hamilton, one of the country's founding fathers, should stay on the $10 bill. They also suggested removing Jackson from the $20 bill, as not only did he own slaves, but he also moved Native Americans from their land. In the end, Hamilton will stay on the front of the $10 note and, on its reverse, the newly redesigned $10 bill will honour another five women - Lucretia Mott, Sojourner Truth, Susan B. Anthony, Elizabeth Cady Stanton and Alice Paul - the leaders of the suffrage movement.

Glossary

to feature (v) apparire, presentare

19. Which of the following statements is correct?

A. ☐ Harriet Tubman was not a famous woman.
B. ☐ Harriet Tubman will be the first woman to appear on a US currency note.
C. ☐ Andrew Jackson was an anti-slavery activist.
D. ☐ Andrew Jackson's image will no longer appear on the $20 bill.

---

20. The expression 'anti-slavery activist' (line 4) means:

A. ☐ a person whose ideas are against any form of slavery and submission.
B. ☐ a person who used to be a slave.
C. ☐ a slaveholder.
D. ☐ a person who holds slaves but who fights for their freedom.

---

21. Harriet Tubman:

A. ☐ was never a slave in her life.
B. ☐ helped to lead other slaves from Canada to the Northern states.
C. ☐ often returned to the North to help lead other slaves to safety.
D. ☐ also fought for women's right to vote.

---

22. Whan was Harriet Tubman born?

A. ☐ She was born in 1861.
B. ☐ She was born in 1822.
C. ☐ She was born in 1865.
D. ☐ She was born in 1832.

---

23. What did American people do?

A. ☐ They suggested removing Jackson from the $10 bill.
B. ☐ They suggested removing Hamilton from the $10 bill.
C. ☐ They suggested keeping Jackson from the $20 bill.
D. ☐ They suggested removing Jackson from the $20 bill.

---

24. Are the following statements **true** or **false**? Tick as appropriate.

		True	False
a	Hamilton will stay on the reverse of the $10 note.	☐	☐
b	The leaders of the suffrage movement were four women.	☐	☐
c	The $10 bill has been completely redesigned.	☐	☐

A2 Task 5 | *True / False / Not Given* questions

Read the following text. Are sentences **(25-30)** *True, False or Not Given in the text? Put a cross (X) in the correct box.*

SOAP OPERAS

Do you like watching TV? If so, what's your favourite TV programme? Some people love watching game shows, others like talk shows, but the most popular TV programmes in Italy are actually soap operas. In the early days of TV, soap operas were often on during the day and aimed at entertaining housewives, probably doing the washing or ironing. Washing powder companies would advertise their products during the breaks or even sponsor the drama, hence the word 'soap'.

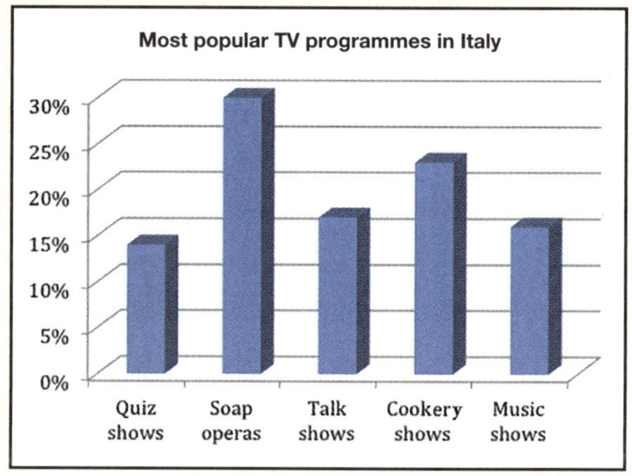

The word 'opera' reflected the fact that many of these dramas are often an exaggeration of real life. Several different storylines go on at the same time and continue over several shows, while the same cast members appear in every show, which is usually shown on the same day and at the same time every week. Soap operas are stories told over an extended period of time, with a storyline affecting several characters and interconnecting with other stories.

During the 1980s, soap operas such as *Dallas*, *Knots Landing*, *Dynasty*, and *Falcon Crest* were shown to adoring fans. Focusing on business conflicts and wealthy families, their sets were as extravagant as the clothes that the actors wore. Filming a soap opera requires plenty of improvisation and quick thinking by the actors. So are you a soap opera fan, or do you hate them as much as many other people do?

		True	False	Not given
25.	People don't like watching TV in Italy.	☐	☐	☐
26.	The word soap in soap opera refers to washing powder used by housewives to do the washing.	☐	☐	☐
27.	The word opera in soap opera refers to the classical singing you hear in the dramas.	☐	☐	☐
28.	Soap operas have lots of continuing storylines happening over a few shows.	☐	☐	☐
29.	There are usually two or three characters in the storyline.	☐	☐	☐
30.	It takes five months to write two different storylines.	☐	☐	☐

Test 6

Section 2 – LISTENING COMPREHENSION

A1 Task 1 | Matching names to pictures

Listen to Yavor describing a picture of the equipment he and his friends need to play sport. For questions **1-5**, *write the owners' names in the boxes. The first one* (**0**) *is an example.*

You will hear the recording twice. You will have 20 seconds at the end of the second recording to complete your answers. You now have 20 seconds to look at the task.

A1 Task 2 | Multiple matching with pictures

Listen to some people talking about their favourite type of books. While listening, match the pictures (**A-H**) *with the people's names* (**6-10**). *Write your answers in the boxes. There are two pictures that you do not need. The first one* (**0**) *is an example.*

You will hear the recording twice. You will have 20 seconds at the end of the second recording to complete your answers. You now have 20 seconds to look at the task.

A.

B.

C.

D.

E.

F.

G.

H.

0 *Adele*	6. Charlie	7. Federica	8. Esther	9. Holly	10. Milton
D	....	....	....	....	....

Test 6

A1 Task 3 | Four-option multiple choice

Listen to two friends, Marylin and Jessica, making arrangements to go to a new restaurant together. While listening, choose the correct answer (**A**, **B**, **C** *or* **D**) *for questions* **11-15**. *Put a cross (☒) in the correct box. Only one answer is correct. The first one* (**0**) *is an example.*

You will hear the recording twice. You will have 20 seconds at the end of the second recording to complete your answers. You now have 20 seconds to look at the task.

Example

0

The new restaurant serves

A. ☐ Mexican food.
B. ☒ Italian food.
C. ☐ Greek food.
D. ☐ Indian food.

11. The restaurant opened

A. ☐ three weeks ago.
B. ☐ two weeks ago.
C. ☐ one week ago.
D. ☐ four weeks ago.

12. The food was

A. ☐ really tasty.
B. ☐ tasty.
C. ☐ not so tasty, especially the pizza.
D. ☐ not so tasty, especially the pasta.

13. Eva

A. ☐ had a problem with the dessert.
B. ☐ said that pasta was great.
C. ☐ found the pizza very tasty.
D. ☐ had a problem with the pasta.

14. After the meal, Jessica went

A. ☐ to the doctor's.
B. ☐ to the café with Eva.
C. ☐ to her house.
D. ☐ to the shopping mall with Eva.

15. In the end, they spent

A. ☐ £20.
B. ☐ £40.
C. ☐ £50.
D. ☐ £30.

A2 Task 4 | Four-option multiple choice

You will hear five short conversations. There is one question for each conversation. While listening, choose the correct answer (**A, B, C** *or* **D**) *for questions* **16-20**. *Put a cross* (X) *in the correct box. Only one answer is correct. The first one* (**0**) *is an example.*

You will hear the recording twice. You will have 20 seconds at the end of the second recording to complete your answers. You now have 20 seconds to look at the task.

Example

0 What will the speakers buy Jacqueline?

A. ☐	B. ☒	C. ☐	D. ☐

16. What will Chris get for his birthday?

A. ☐	B. ☐	C. ☐	D. ☐

17. What does Mr Haffman look like?

A. ☐	B. ☐	C. ☐	D. ☐

18. Where is the man going to plant the tree?

A. ☐	**B.** ☐	**C.** ☐	**D.** ☐

19. Where is the mop and bucket?

A. ☐	**B.** ☐	**C.** ☐	**D.** ☐

20. What has John got?

A. ☐	**B.** ☐	**C.** ☐	**D.** ☐

A2 Task 5 | Matching

Listen to Jenny talking to her friend Alex about a recent trip to Italy. What did each of her family members do? While listening, choose the activity **(A-H)** *done by each of the family member* **(21-25)**. *Write your answers in the boxes. There are two activities that you do not need. The first one* **(0)** *is an example.*

You will hear the recording twice. You will have 20 seconds at the end of the second recording to complete your answers. You now have 20 seconds to look at the task.

Example

0 [F] Frank

People

21. ☐ Jenny
22. ☐ dad
23. ☐ brother
24. ☐ sister
25. ☐ mum

Activities

A. reading
B. windsurfing
C. shopping
D. taking photos
E. sightseeing
F. swimming
G. go-karting
H. snorkelling

A2 Task 6 | Gap-fill (monologue or dialogue)

8 *Listen to Max asking his friend Sarah some information about his trip to Manchester. Use a maximum of 4 words to complete each sentence* (**26-30**). *The first one* (**0**) *is an example.*

You will hear the recording twice. You will have 20 seconds at the end of the second recording to complete your answers. You now have 20 seconds to look at the task.

My trip to Manchester!

When: (**0**) ......October......

Temperature in autumn about: (**26**) ....

Will need to wear: (**27**) ....

Name of the train station in London: (**28**) ....

Cost of train: £ (**29**) ....

Take Sarah some: (**30**) ....

SELF-EVALUATION

Section 1 - Reading Comprehension		Section 2 - Listening Comprehension	
Task 1 score .../7	Total score .../30	Task 1 score .../5	Total score .../30
Task 2 score .../5		Task 2 score .../5	
Task 3 score .../6		Task 3 score .../5	
Task 4 score .../6		Task 4 score .../5	
Task 5 score .../6		Task 5 score .../5	
		Task 6 score .../5	
		FINAL SCORE .../60	

Ho trovato la prova: ☐ Difficile ☐ Più semplice di quanto pensassi ☐ Adeguata alle mie aspettative e capacità ☐ Altro

Test 7

Section 1 – READING COMPREHENSION

A1 Task 1 | Missing information (one to four words)

Read the following poster for a summer resort. For questions **1-7**, *write the missing information. Use a maximum of 4 words.*

The first one (**0**) *is an example.*

0	*What is the camp's name?*	Holiday Inn
1.	What is the maximum age you can take part in the resort?	....
2.	What morning activities are offered?	.... and ....
3.	What afternoon activities are offered?	.... and ....
4.	What evening activities are offered?	.... and ....
5.	What is the resort's daily cost?	£ .... per day
6.	What time does the resort close?	At .... pm
7.	What number should you dial for further information?	....

A1 Task 2 | Matching opinions to statements

Read some customers' opinions (**8-12**) *about travelling: match them with the sentences* (**A-G**). *There is one sentence you do not need. Write your answers in the boxes.*

The first one (**0**) *is an example.*

0	*"... In order to create the false impression that they are as rich as others, poor people save money for travelling. They work hard and save that money in order to feel and show others they are rich...."* *Yavor – Sofia, Bulgaria*	A
8.	"... You could use money to feed many people in need. It can also be used to invest in a home, help a family member or help out in the community. Time spent travelling could be used to do so many other worthy things..." *Simon – Antibes, France*	....
9.	"... We are and we will pay for the effects of this pollution in our environment. Planes are worse than most other forms of transport in terms of the impact of greenhouse gases per passenger mile..." *Blanche – Berne, Switzerland*	....
10.	"... I hate the whole process from packing to planes. Holidays are boring, with people lying on a sun bed for hours. I'm well read and happy to find out about cultures from the comfort of my armchair." *Victoria – Helsinki, Finland*	....
11.	"... Going to another country, by extension, is often a true eye opener and reduces prejudices and boundaries." *Caroline – Belfast, UK*	....
12.	"... It all depends on what the purpose is, if it's to experience culture and to understand our world, then definitely no, as long as the luxuries you use during travel are reasonable." *Millie – Copenhagen, Denmark*	....

A.	*They declare that travelling is something not everybody can afford, but tries to achieve.*
B.	They underline that the value of travelling depends on your goals.
C.	They highlight that travelling leads to a lot of unnecessary pollution.
D.	They think that travelling expands a person's horizon.
E.	They say that travelling won't buy you happiness.
F.	They think that travelling is a waste of money.
G.	They state that they hate travelling.

A2 Task 3 | Matching sentences to notices

*Match the notices (**A-E**) with the sentences (**13-18**). You can use a notice more than once. Write your answers in the boxes.*

*The first one (**0**) is an example.*

A

C

D

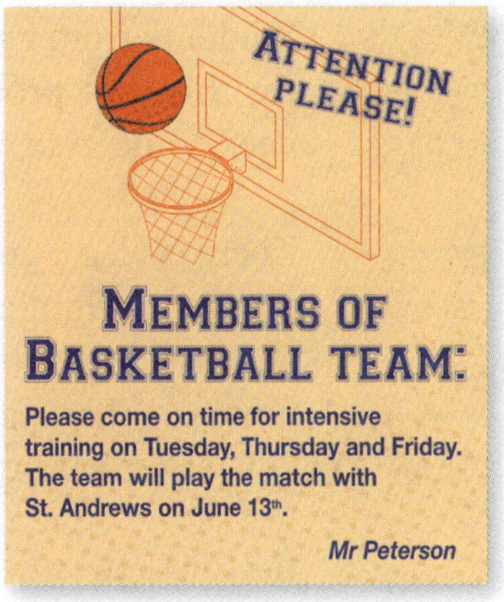

B

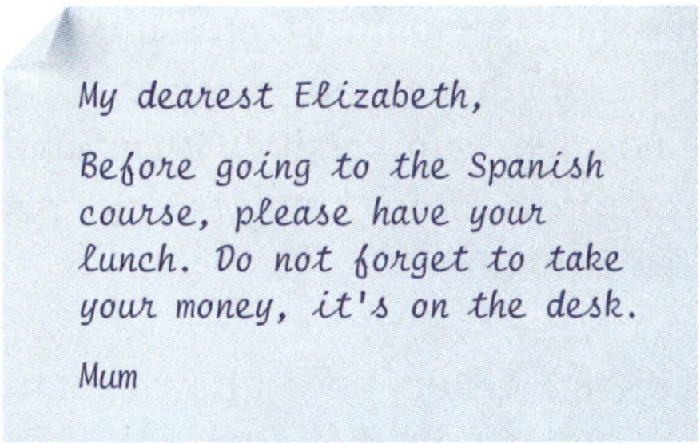

E

0	*This notice says that the lift is broken or does not work.*	E
13.	This notice says that only customers have access to the toilets.	....
14.	This notice says that it is important to have lunch before going to the Spanish course.	....
15.	This notice asks basketball players to get to the practice session on time.	....
16.	This notice says that something has just been painted.	....
17.	This notice reminds Elizabeth to take the money from her desk.	....
18.	This notice is from Mr Peterson.	....

A2 Task 4 | Multiple choice questions

Read the following text, then answer questions **19-24**.

Secondary education in Britain

Students from around the world **enrol** at British universities. There are many reasons for this, but probably the most prominent is that people have understood that you need to be able to speak English to get anywhere these days.

There is also a great deal of frustration with the Italian education system. Many parents see their bright and intelligent children **struggling** with huge amounts of homework and constant, humiliating, 'interrogation'-style tests. The British education system, however, has its negative aspects too, so don't **be deceived**. Fiercely competitive, education in Great Britain is often **elitist** and discriminatory.

In 1991, the British government introduced SATs, or Standard Assessment Tests: these are **compulsory** national tests for primary school pupils. At the age of 16, students take their GCSEs (General Certificate of Secondary Education), and at 18 their A-level exams. These exams put a huge amount of pressure on students, especially A-levels, whose results determine whether or not you are accepted into university. In addition, many young people now leave university with around £27,000 of debt. So it's perhaps not surprising that depression in young people, particularly teenagers, is a serious problem in the United Kingdom.

So, before you decide to abandon Italy and its rich history and culture (not to mention the sun!) remember that the grass isn't always greener on the other side of the **fence** – after all, the British education system can be just as problematic as the Italian system.

Glossary

to enroll (v) iscriversi
to struggle (v) combattere
to be deceived (v) essere illusi
elitist (a) elitario
compulsory (a) obbligatorio
fence (n) staccionata

19. Are the following statements **true** or **false**? Tick as appropriate.

		True	False
a	British universities don't attract Italian students.		
b	The author understands why many parents consider the opportunity of sending their children to secondary schools in the UK.		
c	It is not necessary to be able to communicate well in English to get anywhere these days.		

20. According to the text, many Italian parents think that:

A. ☐ their kids are bright and intelligent, but struggling with mountains of homework.
B. ☐ their kids are not-so-fairly evaluated.
C. ☐ the Italian system works perfectly well.
D. ☐ 'interrogation'-style tests are really useful.

21. The British education system:

A. ☐ is perfect.
B. ☐ encourages students to study.
C. ☐ is similar to the American education system.
D. ☐ has positive aspects as well as negative ones.

22. Education in Britain:

A. ☐ does not make any discriminations between young students.
B. ☐ makes use of 'interrogation'-style tests.
C. ☐ makes use of standardized national tests.
D. ☐ Both options B and C are correct.

23. GCSEs (General Certificate of Secondary Education) and A-level exams:

A. ☐ are taken when students are aged 16 (the earlier) and 18 (the second).
B. ☐ are both taken when students are aged 16.
C. ☐ are increasingly easier each year.
D. ☐ none of the other answers provided is correct.

24. The text above is most probably:

A. ☐ an essay.
B. ☐ a biography.
C. ☐ a divulgative article.
D. ☐ an extract from a novel.

A2 Task 5 | *True / False / Not Given* questions

Read the following text. Are sentences **25-30** *True, False or Not Given in the text? Put a cross (X) in the correct box.*

What does your favourite ice cream flavour say about you?

We all love ice cream, don't we? It's the perfect treat for any season. You can cool off with a scoop of your favourite ice cream in the summer, and in the winter enjoy a slice of hot pie with ice cream. It's simple to make and serve, making it a regular feature at dinners, parties and other events. When you're sad or just a bit down, a big bowl of ice cream will certainly cheer you up. Ice cream can be served in a cup or in a cone, which means you can take your favourite frozen treat wherever you go. So you just have one important decision to make. What flavour of ice cream will you choose? You could go for a classic vanilla, or how about something a little more sophisticated, like pistachio? Your favourite ice cream flavour can say a lot about you. Those who like vanilla ice cream usually appreciate good quality and minimalism, for example. It means you aren't an anxious or stressed person and you find peace in everyday things, and enjoy living in the moment. If caramel ice cream is your favourite, however, you most probably enjoy yoga or meditation, and do a job that challenges you. Caramel ice cream lovers love cats too and their wardrobe probably includes a lot of black things. And finally, we have pistachio lovers who might initially seem reserved, but really have a strong, unique personality, who are also creative and complex. Nothing beats the cool, creamy and sweet taste of ice cream on a sizzling summer's day.

		True	False	Not given
25.	When it's hot, eating an ice cream is the best way to feel less sad.	☐	☐	☐
26.	Ice cream can bring many benefits to our body.	☐	☐	☐
27.	If you like vanilla ice cream, you feel very stressed.	☐	☐	☐
28.	Chocolate ice cream lovers are always open to experience new things.	☐	☐	☐
29.	Coffee ice cream is for those people who like to be on their own, reading a book.	☐	☐	☐
30.	Caramel, strawberry and vanilla are the least favourite ice cream flavours in Japan.	☐	☐	☐

Test 7

Section 2 – LISTENING COMPREHENSION

A1 Task 1 | Matching names to pictures

Listen to Jayden describing a picture of his colleagues. For questions **1-5**, *write the colleagues' names in the boxes. The first one* (**0**) *is an example.*

You will hear the recording twice. You will have 20 seconds at the end of the second recording to complete your answers. You now have 20 seconds to look at the task.

A1 Task 2 | Multiple matching with pictures

*Listen to some people talking about the clothes they like to wear. While listening, match the pictures (**A-H**) with the people's names (**6-10**). Write your answers in the boxes. There are two pictures that you do not need. The first one (**0**) is an example.*

You will hear the recording twice. You will have 20 seconds at the end of the second recording to complete your answers. You now have 20 seconds to look at the task.

A.

B.

C.

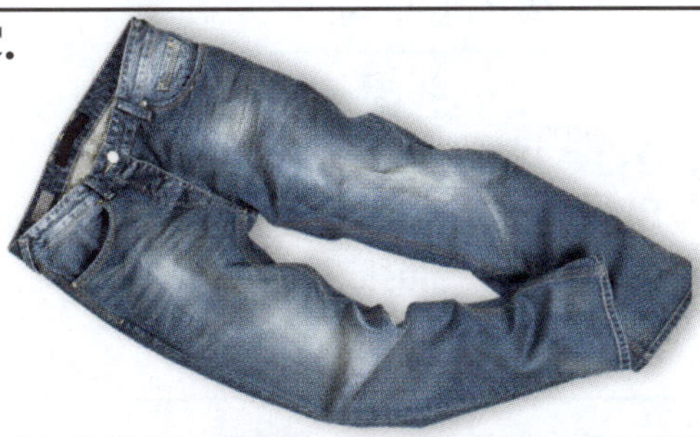

D.

E.

F.

G.

H.

0 *Mia*	**6. Amelia**	**7. Eve**	**8. Jacob**	**9. Adam**	**10. Carter**
D	....	....	....	....	....

Test 7

A1 Task 3 | Four-option multiple choice

Listen to the conversation between Hugo and his friend Lucille about the things they do in their free time. While listening, choose the correct answer (**A**, **B**, **C** *or* **D**) *for questions* **11-15**. *Put a cross* (X) *in the correct box. Only one answer is correct. The first one* (**0**) *is an example.*

You will hear the recording twice. You will have 20 seconds at the end of the second recording to complete your answers. You now have 20 seconds to look at the task.

Example

0

Hugo asks Lucille to come with him to

A. ☐ the gym.
B. ☒ a concert.
C. ☐ a meeting.
D. ☐ school.

11. Lucille loves

A. ☐ pop music.
B. ☐ classical music.
C. ☐ rock music.
D. ☐ folk music.

---

12. Lucille has a horse riding competition

A. ☐ on Saturday.
B. ☐ earlier this month.
C. ☐ at the end of the month.
D. ☐ at the end of the year.

---

13. Hugo prefers

A. ☐ going to the cinema.
B. ☐ playing videogames.
C. ☐ studying.
D. ☐ horse riding.

---

14. Lucille

A. ☐ loves videogames.
B. ☐ quite loves videogames.
C. ☐ really likes videogames.
D. ☐ can't stand videogames.

---

15. Hugo can play

A. ☐ the drums.
B. ☐ the piano.
C. ☐ the saxophone.
D. ☐ the electric guitar.

A2 Task 4 | Four-option multiple choice

*You will hear five short conversations. There is one question for each conversation. While listening, choose the correct answer (**A, B, C** or **D**) for questions **16-20**. Put a cross (X) in the correct box. Only one answer is correct. The first one (**0**) is an example.*

You will hear the recording twice. You will have 20 seconds at the end of the second recording to complete your answers. You now have 20 seconds to look at the task.

Example

0 What will the speakers buy Jacqueline?

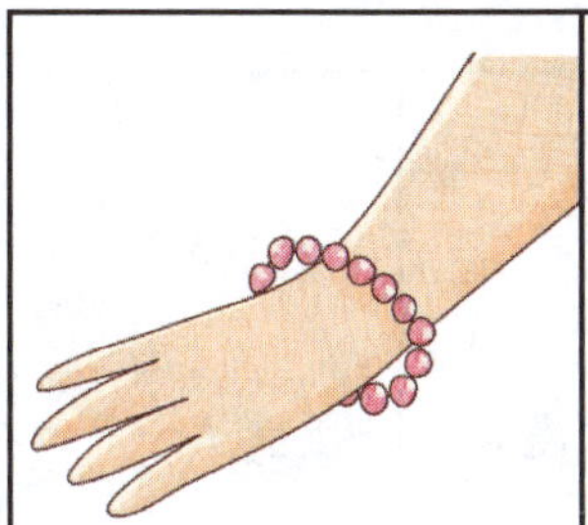			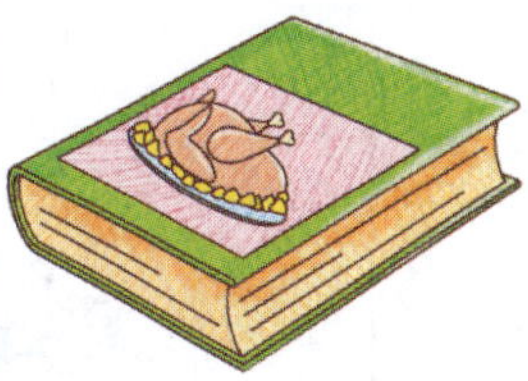
A. ☐	**B.** ☒	**C.** ☐	**D.** ☐

16. What is the woman going to buy?

A. ☐	**B.** ☐	**C.** ☐	**D.** ☐

17. What colour dress does Angie decide to take?

A. ☐	**B.** ☐	**C.** ☐	**D.** ☐

18. Which dessert does the customer choose for dinner?

A. ☐	**B.** ☐	**C.** ☐	**D.** ☐

19. Which toy does George give up?

			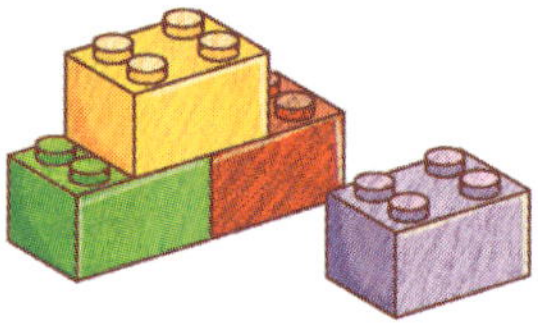
A. ☐	**B.** ☐	**C.** ☐	**D.** ☐

20. Where does the couple decide to go on holiday?

A. ☐	**B.** ☐	**C.** ☐	**D.** ☐

A2 Task 5 | Matching

Listen to Lucas talking to a friend about his health problems. What happened to him during each day of the week? While listening, choose the health problem **(A-H)** *for each day of the week* **(21-25)**. *Write your answers in the boxes. There are two activities that you do not need. The first one* **(0)** *is an example.*

You will hear the recording twice. You will have 20 seconds at the end of the second recording to complete your answers. You now have 20 seconds to look at the task.

Example

0 [D] Sunday

Day of the week

21. ☐ Monday
22. ☐ Tuesday
23. ☐ Wednesday
24. ☐ Thursday
25. ☐ Friday

Health problem

A. stomach ache
B. earache
C. broken leg
D. sore throat
E. flu
F. toothache
G. pain in the neck
H. insect bite

Test 7

A2 Task 6 | Gap-fill (monologue or dialogue)

Listen to a circus manager talking about life in a circus. Use a maximum of 4 words to complete each sentence **(26-30)**. *The first one* **(0)** *is an example.*

You will hear the recording twice. You will have 20 seconds at the end of the second recording to complete your answers. You now have 20 seconds to look at the task.

The big tent!

A circus is usually circular and **(0)** ...surrounded by seats... for spectators.

At the circus you can see performances of gymnasts, **(26)** .... and performing animals.

The first modern circus was in London in **(27)** ....

Performers have to **(28)** ....out of entertaining.

Artists at the circus use **(29)** .... while hanging from a wire.

The circus manager started to do **(30)** .... but then he changed his mind.

SELF-EVALUATION

Section 1 – Reading Comprehension		Section 2 – Listening Comprehension	
Task 1 score .../7	Total score .../30	Task 1 score .../5	Total score .../30
Task 2 score .../5		Task 2 score .../5	
Task 3 score .../6		Task 3 score .../5	
Task 4 score .../6		Task 4 score .../5	
Task 5 score .../6		Task 5 score .../5	
		Task 6 score .../5	
		FINAL SCORE .../60	

Ho trovato la prova: ☐ Difficile ☐ Più semplice di quanto pensassi ☐ Adeguata alle mie aspettative e capacità ☐ Altro

Test 8

Section 1 – READING COMPREHENSION

A1 Task 1 | Missing information (one to four words)

Read the following invitation for a beach party. For questions **1-7**, *write the missing information. Use a maximum of 4 words.*

The first one (**0**) *is an example.*

0	*Who is turning 11 soon?*	Ethan
1.	What is Ethan celebrating?	His ....
2.	When does the birthday party take place?	On ....
3.	What is the beach's name?	.... Beach
4.	What is the beach's address?	....
5.	What should you remember to wear?	.... and lots of ....
6.	What are they going to cook?	....
7.	What number should you dial for further information?	....

A1 Task 2 | Matching opinions to statements

Read some customers' opinions **(8-12)** *about an amusement park: match them with the sentences* **(A-G)**. *There is one sentence you do not need. Write your answers in the boxes.*

The first one **(0)** *is an example.*

0	*"... I've had the pleasure of visiting this establishment on multiple occasions. Plenty of parking and just a short drive from downtown Boulder, which is a plus."* *Sasha B. – Boulder, CO*	D ....
8.	"... This place is awesome! We went with family and we spent a good couple of hours here, had a great time! The mini-golf course is fun and well planned! Totally coming back." *Allie H. – Monterey, CA*	....
9.	"... Great if you are planning to spend about 1.5 hours here. There are lots of games to play inside and we enjoyed riding the go-karts very much! Overall, it's a fantastic place to spend an afternoon!" *Dan N. – Louisville, KY*	....
10.	"... The prices are decent, the food is good – just what you'd expect from a fun park, and the staff are always very friendly and helpful, no matter how crazy it is inside." *Christian M. – Englewood, CO*	....
11.	"... Had a very bad experience with the manager: he yelled at my children. Furthermore, the place is a complete dirty disaster, and some of the staff were extremely rude. Horrible service, a total waste of money and time!" *Michael H. – Denver, CO*	....
12.	"... Always a great time whether it's with kids or adults. Well maintained facility. I went here with my two boys and my best friend for a round of mini golf. We had a very nice time! The course was not as expensive as some other places." *Sarah H. – Lakewood, CO*	....

A.	They declare that the entrance tickets were too expensive.
B.	They say that they will definitely go back to the amusement park.
C.	They underline that the food was good and that the staff was friendly and helpful.
D.	*They say that the park is not far from the city centre and that there is plenty of parking.*
E.	They highlight that the staff was unpleasant and that the service was awful.
F.	They think that the go-karts rides were very enjoyable.
G.	They think that visiting this park is fun for both adults and children.

A2 Task 3 | Matching sentences to notices

Match the notices (**A-E**) *with the sentences* (**13-18**). *You can use a notice more than once. Write your answers in the boxes.*

The first one (**0**) *is an example.*

A

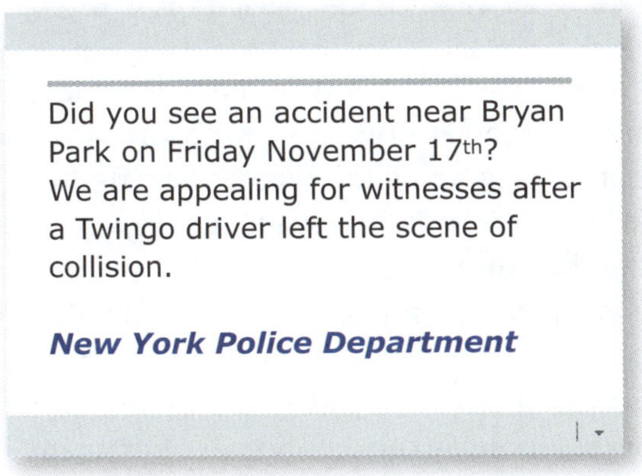

C

B

D

E

0	*This notice says that it is prohibited to pass without stopping.*	B
13.	This notice says that there has been an accident recently.	....
14.	This notice can be found in a shopping mall.	....
15.	This notice is from the New York Police Department.	....
16.	This notice says that you will get a 10% discount if you spend at least £50.	....
17.	This notice reminds you that eating and drinking is forbidden in that place.	....
18.	This notice says it is important to wear special shoes.	....

A2 Task 4 | Multiple choice questions

Read the following text, then answer questions **19-24**.

To bidet, or not to bidet?

The British are completely confused by one French invention – the bidet. Dating back to the late 17th century, most middle-aged Britons have probably never set eyes on a bidet unless they've stayed in an expensive hotel, where they find one in the bathroom. Then of course there's the story of the Italian student studying in the UK, who when asked if there was anything they didn't like, there is always one aspect of British culture that they have problems with from day one: it was the notable absence of a bidet in the bathroom.

Young people staying in host families are particularly afflicted by this problem, as bidets are usually only found in larger, more luxurious homes. For many British people, the bidet is still, strangely, regarded as an upper-class object. Many bidet-lovers hate being somewhere without one.

And that takes us to the subject of hygiene. Many would say that Italian households have a higher standard of cleanliness than you would find in the UK. One young British woman with a particularly house-proud mother was made to do the chores when she was young, but even she had to adapt when she first lived in Italy. At her daughter's nursery, all the parents used to meet once a month to give the place a thorough clean.

She tells us the story of having to clean a classroom one day. Anxious to make a good impression, she scrubbed every inch of the room. Nearing the end of the morning, an Italian mum looked in and said, 'Oh, Lucy. You've forgotten to do the top of the skirting board.' 'Oh, yes, silly me!' she answered, thinking, 'What? The top of the skirting board? Whoever cleans that?' Italians do apparently!

19. Italian students studying in the UK:

A. ☐ complain about the absence of a bidet in the bathroom.
B. ☐ are told by the author to tell them about the aspects they liked most.
C. ☐ have nothing to complain of.
D. ☐ usually visit England for quite a long time.

20. The term 'upper-class' (line 10) means:

A. ☐ proletarian.
B. ☐ inferior.
C. ☐ noble.
D. ☐ none of the other answers provided is correct.

21. One British woman:

A. ☐ didn't have to adapt to Italian habits.
B. ☐ had a very house-proud mother.
C. ☐ had a new-born baby boy.
D. ☐ thought that the Germans were the inventors of the bidet.

22. Which of the following is a synonym of the term 'chores' (line 14)?

A. ☐ Tribulation.
B. ☐ Burden.
C. ☐ Trial.
D. ☐ Housework.

23. At the British woman's daughter's nursery:

A. ☐ all the parents used to meet ten times a year to give the place a thorough clean.
B. ☐ all the parents used to meet two times a semester to give the place a thorough clean.
C. ☐ all the parents used to meet twelve times a year to give the place a thorough clean.
D. ☐ all the parents used to meet now and then to give the place a thorough clean.

24. The 'skirting board' (line 21):

A. ☐ is part of a desk.
B. ☐ is part of a chair.
C. ☐ is part of the wall.
D. ☐ is part of the blackboard.

A2 Task 5 | *True / False / Not Given* questions

*Read the following text. Are sentences (**25–30**) True, False or Not Given in the text? Put a cross (X) in the correct box.*

Most popular dog breeds

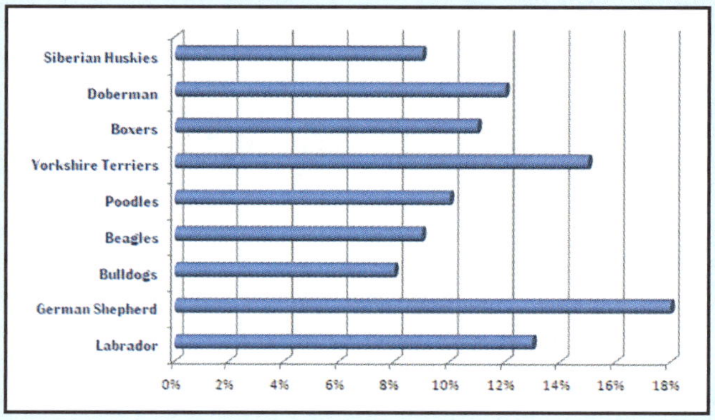

Everyone likes dogs, don't they? But what are the most popular dog breeds?

- The loyal Labrador Retriever has been the most popular dog breed in the United States for 23 years. These dogs are gentle and have a people-pleasing personality making them excellent for therapy, search-and-rescue and families.
- Then there's the German Shepherd which is famous for its use in law enforcement and the military. They are also very loyal family dogs.
- Another possible favourite is the Beagle hound which comes in three colour varieties: tricolour, red-and-white and lemon. As long ago as the 1500s, English hunters used packs of beagles to hunt smaller game like foxes and rabbits. Of course, the most famous Beagle has to be Snoopy, Charlie Brown's dog in the Peanuts comics.
- The Bulldog, known for its stocky build and wide, wrinkly face, is one of the most recognizable dog breeds and its name refers to the breed's original use in bull baiting, which was banned in England by 1835. Some families like having a Bulldog because of its relaxed temperament and minimal need of grooming and exercise.
- There are those who prefer a smaller dog like the Yorkshire Terrier, seen today as a purse dog. Weighing little more than 7 pounds, they have long, silky blue-and-tan coats.
- What about the Poodle? Originating in Germany where hunters used the dogs as water retrievers, these dogs come in three sizes and can be a number of different colours. So which breed of dog will you choose to welcome to your home?

		True	False	Not given
25.	*Labradors* are trained as therapy or service dogs because of their loving personality.	☐	☐	☐
26.	More people in New Zealand own *Labrador Retrievers* than any other breed.	☐	☐	☐
27.	*German Shepherds* are often the preferred breed for police and military roles.	☐	☐	☐
28.	It is not possible to find a yellow *Beagle*.	☐	☐	☐
29.	The *Bulldog* name has nothing to do with the baiting of bulls.	☐	☐	☐
30.	The *Yorkshire Terrier* is so small that you can carry it in a bag.	☐	☐	☐

Test 8

Section 2 – LISTENING COMPREHENSION

A1 Task 1 | Matching names to pictures

Listen to Brittany describing a picture of the souvenirs she bought for her family. For questions (**1-5**)*, write the family members' names in the boxes. The first one* (**0**) *is an example.*

You will hear the recording twice. You will have 20 seconds at the end of the second recording to complete your answers. You now have 20 seconds to look at the task.

0 Julia ....

4 ....

5 ....

1 ....

2 ....

3 ....

A1 Task 2 | Multiple matching with pictures

*Listen to some people talking about the houses they would like to live in. While listening, match the pictures (**A-H**) with the people's names (**6-10**). Write your answers in the boxes. There are two pictures that you do not need. The first one (**0**) is an example.*

You will hear the recording twice. You will have 20 seconds at the end of the second recording to complete your answers. You now have 20 seconds to look at the task.

A

B

C

D

E

F

G

H

0 ***Alani***	**6. Henk**	**7. Angelina**	**8. Solomon**	**9. Audrey**	**10. Ricky**
H	....	....	....	....	....

A1 Task 3 | Four-option multiple choice

Listen to Sybil and her cousin Denzel talking about computers. While listening, choose the correct answer (**A**, **B**, **C** *or* **D**) *for questions* **11-15**. *Put a cross* (X) *in the correct box. Only one answer is correct. The first one* (**0**) *is an example.*

You will hear the recording twice. You will have 20 seconds at the end of the second recording to complete your answers. You now have 20 seconds to look at the task.

Example

0

Sybil needs

A. ☐ a new project.
B. ☐ a new pen.
C. ☒ a new computer.
D. ☐ some paper.

11. Sybil uses her smartphone to

A. ☐ post photos.
B. ☐ check emails.
C. ☐ take photos.
D. ☐ all of the above.

12. A desktop computer won't need

A. ☐ to update software.
B. ☐ to have a big memory.
C. ☐ to recharge the battery.
D. ☐ a monitor.

13. Sybil would like to have

A. ☐ a tablet.
B. ☐ a laptop.
C. ☐ a desktop computer.
D. ☐ a smartphone.

14. Sybil thinks that a laptop would be

A. ☐ heavier.
B. ☐ difficult to carry.
C. ☐ cheaper.
D. ☐ portable.

15. Denzel suggests Sybil to buy a tablet because

A. ☐ she can put it in her bag.
B. ☐ she wants to spend a lot of money.
C. ☐ it's in the sales.
D. ☐ he finds it very useful.

A2 Task 4 | Four-option multiple choice

You will hear five short conversations. There is one question for each conversation. While listening, choose the correct answer (**A**, **B**, **C** *or* **D**) *for questions* **16-20**. *Put a cross* (X) *in the correct box. Only one answer is correct. The first one* (**0**) *is an example.*

You will hear the recording twice. You will have 20 seconds at the end of the second recording to complete your answers. You now have 20 seconds to look at the task.

Example

0 What will the speakers buy Jacqueline?

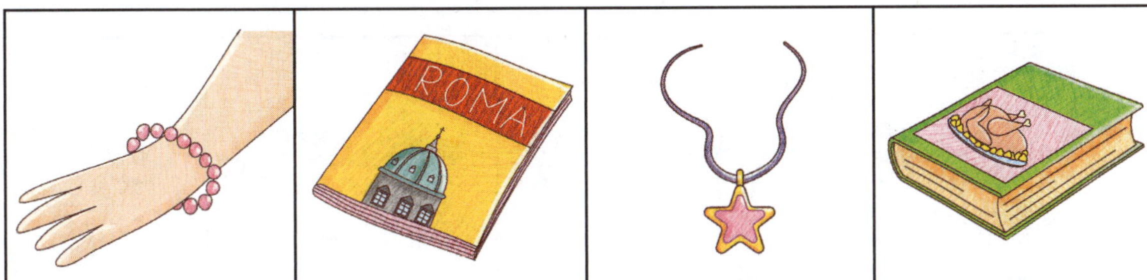

A. ☐	**B.** ☒	**C.** ☐	**D.** ☐

16. What does Danielle need to buy at the supermarket?

A. ☐	**B.** ☐	**C.** ☐	**D.** ☐

17. Where did the girl leave her book?

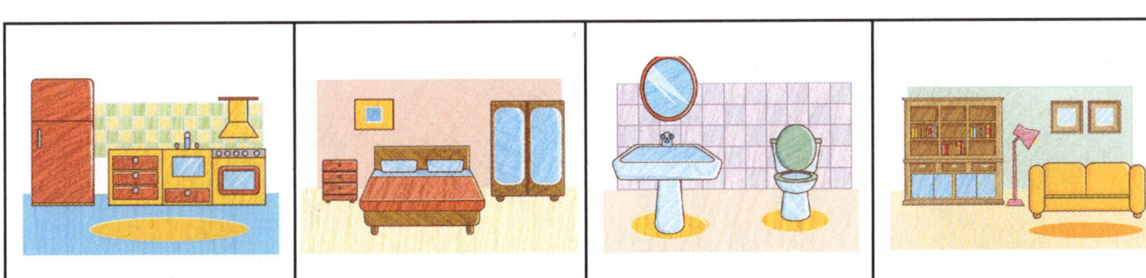

A. ☐	**B.** ☐	**C.** ☐	**D.** ☐

18. What painting does the man want to buy?

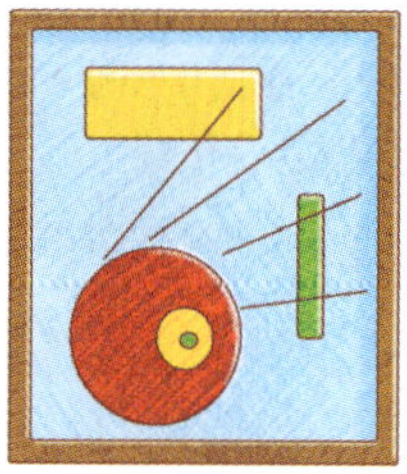			
A. ☐	**B.** ☐	**C.** ☐	**D.** ☐

19. What test is Frederick studying for tomorrow?

A. ☐	**B.** ☐	**C.** ☐	**D.** ☐

20. Where did Julie receive a postcard from?

A. ☐	**B.** ☐	**C.** ☐	**D.** ☐

A2 Task 5 | Matching

Listen to Patrick talking to a friend about the flowers he would like to buy his girl-friends. What flowers would he buy for each girl? While listening, choose the day of the week **(A-H)** *for each health problem* **(21-25)**. *Write your answers in the boxes. There are two activities that you do not need. The first one* **(0)** *is an example.*

You will hear the recording twice. You will have 20 seconds at the end of the second recording to complete your answers. You now have 20 seconds to look at the task.

Example

0 ☐ E Trisha

Friends

21. ☐ Veronique

22. ☐ Zora

23. ☐ Leonie

24. ☐ Fran

25. ☐ Marika

Flower

A. tulips

B. orchids

C. roses

D. daisies

E. sunflowers

F. violets

G. poppies

H. irises

A2 Task 6 | Gap-fill (monologue or dialogue)

Listen to Harper talking to a friend about her passion for tiny houses. Use a maximum of 4 words to complete each sentence (**26-30**). *The first one* (**0**) *is an example.*

You will hear the recording twice. You will have 20 seconds at the end of the second recording to complete your answers. You now have 20 seconds to look at the task.

Tiny houses!

Harper is reading an article (**0**) ....in a magazine.... about tiny houses.

In Jessica's flat there are (**26**) .... for her clothes.

Harper always watches (**27**) .... dedicated to this style.

If you have a tiny home you don't have to (**28**) .... to travel.

Some tiny homes have (**29**) .... and are environmentally friendly.

As you have less space in the house, tidying up will only take (**30**) ....

SELF-EVALUATION

Section 1 - Reading Comprehension		Section 2 - Listening Comprehension	
Task 1 score .../7	Total score .../30	Task 1 score .../5	Total score .../30
Task 2 score .../5		Task 2 score .../5	
Task 3 score .../6		Task 3 score .../5	
Task 4 score .../6		Task 4 score .../5	
Task 5 score .../6		Task 5 score .../5	
		Task 6 score .../5	
		FINAL SCORE .../60	

Ho trovato la prova: ☐ Difficile ☐ Più semplice di quanto pensassi ☐ Adeguata alle mie aspettative e capacità ☐ Altro

EXTRA SECTION 1

LANGUAGE IN USE

A2 Task 1 | Gap-fill (multiple choice)

Read the following text. Choose the best word (**A**, **B** *or* **C**) *for each space* (**1-5**).
Put a cross (X) *in the correct box.*

The first one (**0**) *is an example.*

Example

0 **A.** ☐ with **B.** ☒ through **C.** ☐ on

Where dreams come true

If you have never visited a theme park with your children, then expect to be amazed! We're talking about the magical little ways the parks will look different when you can see them (**0**) ...through... the eyes of a child. Disney's rich details cover every surface of the park.

Many of the most interesting and enchanting details in the Disney parks are around the eye level of (**1**) .... smallest guests, while others are directly beneath your feet, where children are more likely **to spot** them on the ground. If your children have their eyes **glued to the ground**, give them time. Instead, get down to their level to see what they're (**2**) .... at. The streets around The Flying Carpets of Aladdin in Magic Kingdom have gems and coins in them. Planets and moons are featured in the pavement around Mission Space in Epcot.

Walt Disney Parks and Resorts give millions of guests each year the chance (**3**) .... spend time with their families and friends, making memories that last a lifetime. Disney offers something to look at no matter where your eye level falls. Disney's famous characters take on a whole new life when you have children (**4**) .... you.

Disney's characters are trained to speak to children. Even the largest characters will do all they can to get down to the child's eye level and offer a gentle **high-five** or warm hug. One (**5**) .... the most magical experiences you can have is watching a child rush to greet their favourite princess, fully believing that they're in the presence of real royalty.

1.	**A.** ☐ its	**B.** ☐ her	**C.** ☐ our
2.	**A.** ☐ watching	**B.** ☐ looking	**C.** ☐ flying
3.	**A.** ☐ for	**B.** ☐ to	**C.** ☐ through
4.	**A.** ☐ at	**B.** ☐ along	**C.** ☐ with
5.	**A.** ☐ in	**B.** ☐ of	**C.** ☐ on

Glossary

to spot (v) individuare, riconoscere
glued to the ground incollati al suolo
high-five gesto 'dammi cinque'

A2 Task 2 | Gap-fill (multiple choice)

Read the following text. Choose the best word (**A**, **B** *or* **C**) *for each space* (**6-10**). *Put a cross* (X) *in the correct box.*

The first one (**0**) *is an example.*

Example

0 **A.** ☒ an **B.** ☐ on **C.** ☐ off

DOWN UNDER

Australia is the only country in the world that covers (**0**) ....an....... entire continent, but surprisingly it is the largest island in the world as well! More than 24 million people (**6**) .... in Australia, which are not so many if you consider how big this country is. The majority of the country is desert, which is called the *outback*.

The capital is Canberra, but its largest urban area is Sydney. Another important city is Alice Springs, which is collocated in the (**7**) .... of the *outback*. Tourists come to Alice Springs because they can try different adventure sports in the desert, like camping, mountain biking and walking. You can't miss the experience of flying (**8**) .... the desert in a hot air balloon, a helicopter or a small plane. The first explorers crossed the *outback* using camels.

The first people to live in Australia were the Aborigines, and they've (**9**) .... there for approximately 50,000 years! Today the Aborigines live in the desert areas of the Australian *outback* and they've learnt to survive under these harsh desert conditions.

Australia was first called New Holland because it was discovered by Dutch explorers. Australia's nickname is *Down Under* as it is faraway, but also because it has got unique animals and plants that can't be found anywhere else in the world, such as kangaroos, echidnas, kookaburras and koalas.

The Great Barrier Reef is the biggest (**10**) .... reef in the world. It is made up of more than 3,000 reefs, and there are more than 1,500 species of fish!

The Australian flag has three parts, the Commonwealth Star, the Southern Cross and the Union Jack. Australia is a member of the Commonwealth of Nations, and this means that the head of state is Queen Elizabeth II!

6.	**A.** ☐ alive	**B.** ☐ live	**C.** ☐ life
7.	**A.** ☐ middle	**B.** ☐ half	**C.** ☐ between
8.	**A.** ☐ under	**B.** ☐ in	**C.** ☐ over
9.	**A.** ☐ been	**B.** ☐ gone	**C.** ☐ were
10.	**A.** ☐ local	**B.** ☐ coral	**C.** ☐ choral

A2 Task 3 | Gap-fill (multiple choice)

Read the following text. Choose the best word (**A**, **B** *or* **C**) *for each space* (**11-15**). *Put a cross* (X) *in the correct box.*

The first one (**0**) *is an example.*

Example

0 **A.** ☐ blue **B.** ☐ green **C.** ☒ pink

FLAMINGOES' SECRETS

Have you ever seen the image of a pink bird standing isolated on a white background? Flamingoes are known all over the world for their bright (**0**) .....pink..... feathers, long thin legs, and S-shaped neck. Their favourite dinner includes fish, shrimp, snails, and algae and to get them, it **plunges** its head into the water, twists it upside down, and takes the fish using its upper beak. They are able to run (**11**) .... water, because they are **endowed with** webbed feet, allowing them to gain speed before lifting up into the sky.

Flamingoes build nests for only one egg. The female and the male take turns sitting on the (**12**) .... to keep it warm for about 30 days until the egg **hatches**. Baby flamingoes have white, soft feathers. Both parents feed the newborn flamingo with a fluid produced in their digestive systems.

After five or six days the young flamingo leaves the nest to join other young specimen in small groups but they always return to the parents for food. After about twenty-two days, young flamingoes start to look for food on their own.

Have you ever wondered why flamingoes are able to sleep while standing on one (**13**) .... ? Researchers in Atlanta, USA, say they can stand on just one leg for many hours because of their skeleton structure. The flamingo's **hips** and leg bones are in a special shape and position that give the (**14**) .... balance. The position of the bones in a flamingo means the birds do not need to use so many muscles to **keep still**. Some French biologists suggest that standing on one leg may allow the birds to save energy and conserve more body heat, since they spend a lot of time splashing in cold water.

Another researcher, Dr Geoffrey Michigan, said that it would be very difficult for a human to stay still without (**15**) ...., even for an hour. You could try, if you want to! A man's muscles constantly change to keep us straight and prevent us from falling over.

11.	**A.** ☐ in	**B.** ☐ on	**C.** ☐ under
12.	**A.** ☐ egg	**B.** ☐ male	**C.** ☐ water
13.	**A.** ☐ hand	**B.** ☐ toe	**C.** ☐ leg
14.	**A.** ☐ fish	**B.** ☐ bird	**C.** ☐ insect
15.	**A.** ☐ moving	**B.** ☐ sleeping	**C.** ☐ flying

Glossary

to plunge (v) tuffarsi, lanciarsi in qualcosa
endowed with (a) dotati di
to hatch (v) schiudersi
hips (n) fianchi, anche
to keep still (v) stare fermo

A2 Task 4 | Gap-fill (multiple choice)

Read the following text. Choose the best word (**A**, **B** *or* **C**) *for each space* (**16-20**). *Put a cross* (X) *in the correct box.*

The first one (**0**) *is an example.*

Example

0	**A.** ☐ months	**B.** ☐ days	**C.** ☒ years

BICYCLES

Cycling is a fantastic sport, and bicycles have a long, interesting history. They've been in use for almost two hundred **(0)** ....years.... now, and they have also evolved during that period of time. The first bicycles were completely different from the ones used nowadays, and were not as **(16)** .... as they are now. Bicycles are always fun and they make it really easy to get from one place to another.

When adults started to drive after the 1920s, bikes started to be considered as toys and were used by those who were too young to drive a car; they provide many different benefits compared with motor vehicles, for example: easier parking, access to roads, bike paths and rural trails. In fact, until the arrival of the car, bicycles were mostly used by adults, as practical and efficient means of transportation. Cycling is also useful to reduce pollution, as it requires a lower consumption of fossil fuels, less air or noise pollution, and significantly reduced traffic queues.

Cycling seems to possess a **(17)** .... of qualities that give **(18)** .... in ways that few other sports can do.
It has been demonstrated that aerobic **(19)** .... is one of the greatest predictors of our physical health and that cycling boosts mental health. In fact, our body simply works better when we are physically fit, and people who are physically fit and healthy are generally happier than their unfit and unhealthy similars. As a consequence, depression, anxiety, and stress are generally lower in physically healthy people.
In conclusion, riding on your own is, on one hand, great, on the other, our best times on the bike often involve group rides with **(20)** ....

16.	**A.** ☐ comfortable	**B.** ☐ eatable	**C.** ☐ sociable
17.	**A.** ☐ good	**B.** ☐ number	**C.** ☐ many
18.	**A.** ☐ anxiety	**B.** ☐ sadness	**C.** ☐ happiness
19.	**A.** ☐ exercise	**B.** ☐ gym	**C.** ☐ coach
20.	**A.** ☐ surfers	**B.** ☐ friends	**C.** ☐ drivers

A2 Task 5 | Gap-fill (one word)

Read and complete the following text. For each space (**21-30**) *write the best word to fill the gap. Write only ONE word for each gap.*

The first one (**0**) *is an example.*

Animals in the city

Recently, there have been many reports (**0**) ......in...... newspapers and on TV about big animals coming (**21**) .... towns and cities. There have been bears in Vancouver parks, leopards (**22**) .... the streets of Mumbai and wild pigs in gardens in Berlin. What happens (**23**) .... big animals come into our cities? Is it a good thing or is it dangerous (**24**) .... us and the animals?

Wild animals usually come into cities (**25**) .... look for food. In Cape Town, South Africa, baboons sometimes come into the suburbs. They eat fruit (**26**) .... gardens and go into people's kitchens to find food. Baboons are big animals and sometimes they scare children and fight (**27**) .... pet dogs. Many people do not like (**28**) ...., but the city can be risky for baboons; sometimes, for example, baboons are hurt in car accidents.

The city council in Cape Town has a team (**29**) .... Baboon Monitors. The Monitors have to find baboons in the city and take them (**30**) .... to the savana. This makes the city safer for people and it is healthier for the baboons. The problem is that a lot of baboons will come back to the city to find food again.

A2 Task 6 | Gap-fill (one word)

Read and complete the following text. For each space (**31-40**) *write the best word to fill the gap. Write only ONE word for each gap.*

The first one (**0**) *is an example.*

THE ART OF GRAFFITI

In the 1970s, some young people (**0**) ....in...... New York used ordinary pens to write their names on the big city walls. One (**31**) .... the first taggers was called Pablo, a teenager (**32**) .... a Mexican family. Most people say that Pablo was not his real name. He loved to sign his works with the tag PfM 2507, where PfM was (**33**) .... nickname and meant Pablo from Mexico (as he was proud of his origins) and 2507 was the number of the house (**34**) .... he lived – 2507 Madison Street. His first tags were left on his neighbours' walls when he was only twelve and they were not very happy to see those labels on their building, as they considered them an act of vandalism. Later he started writing his trademark in subway stations when he travelled to school. When the train stopped at a station, he jumped (**35**) ...., wrote his marker on the wall and then jumped back on the train before the doors closed. Pablo inspired other teenagers who began writing (**36**) .... personal tags everywhere on benches, fountains, walls, buses and trains all over New York.

At a certain point some taggers changed their pens with aerosol paints, so their graffiti became bigger and (**37**) .... colourful. Then, in (**38**) .... 1970s and 1980s, aerosol paint graffiti started to become very popular all around the world and appeared for the first time on walls, trains and buses. In the 2000s, a lot of graffiti artists started to create beautiful pictures which represented their inner feelings or beliefs. Some artists were interested in politics and tried (**39**) .... use their pieces of art to make people think about social problems and discrimination (**40**) .... their pictures. On the other hand, for some artists the only aim of their art was making cities more attractive. In South America, street artists brought colour and beauty to grey city walls.

A2 Task 7 | Gap-fill (one word)

Read and complete the following text. For each space (**41-50**) *write the best word to fill the gap. Write only ONE word for each gap.*

The first one (**0**) *is an example.*

A book review

In 2001, the Canadian author Yann Martel published a fiction book entitled *The Life of Pi*, that tells the story of a young teenage boy (**0**) ...from... India, whose name was Pi, who one day finds himself trapped (**41**) .... a tiger on a boat in the Pacific Ocean. This novel, which is the third one (**42**) .... the author Yann Martel, has sold about seven million copies all over the world, has won several prestigious prizes and has been translated (**43**) .... more than forty different languages.

(**44**) .... the start of the book, we read that Pi spent his childhood in Pondicherry, a small district in India. When Pi turns 16, his parents decide to close down their zoo and completely change their lives, moving to Canada. While they are sailing to Canada, the ship sinks because of a terrible storm. Unfortunately, all Pi's family members and the sailors die (**45**) .... the storm, but Pi survives and finds himself in a boat with a hyena, a zebra, an orangutan and a huge tiger. One by one, the animals start to kill and eat (**46**) .... other for survival, and in the end only Pi and the tiger stay alive. Luckily (**47**) .... Pi, there is enough food and water to carry on, but soon the only way to get something to eat every day was catching fish. He also gave food to the tiger (**48**) .... prevent it from killing and eating him because of hunger.

Pi and the tiger spend more than two hundred days together on the lifeboat. They are also able to get (**49**) .... terrible storms and the burning heat of the Pacific sun. They are often hungry and ill. Sometimes, Pi feels sad and lonely, other times he finds comfort in his three religions, until they finally arrive at the coast of Mexico, but you will have to read the book to find (**50**) .... what happens in the end!

A2 Task 8 | Gap-fill (one word)

Read and complete the following text. For each space (**51-60**) *write the best word to fill the gap. Write only ONE word for each gap.*

The first one (**0**) *is an example.*

Guess what?

Today was a really big day **(0)** ....for........ me. The last time I spoke in class was three years ago and it didn't go well. I tried **(51)** .... say the letter 'W' and made that strange sound. Everyone laughed at me and I haven't spoken in class **(52)** .... then. But it's been going really well lately. I've got a great speech therapist and I can use my laptop in class **(53)** .... the time. I've even got an app that turns text into speech! Very cool! And guess what? When I listen to music on my headphones in the background I can speak **(54)** .... stuttering! That's why I agreed to talk at the science fair today. Our project is about using bacteria to eat plastic. Well, I think it's really interesting.

Luke Williams was waiting **(55)** .... the entrance when I arrived. He smiled at me. Then Ryan Colby came **(56)** .... and said, 'Hey, Tom, guess what?' I didn't think. I tried to say, 'What?' and of course got stuck on the 'W' and you can guess what happened then. Ryan Colby and his friends started laughing. So yes, I turned and ran. Very brave! I wasn't going **(57)** .... take part in the presentation, but then I got a text from Dad saying good luck. And I thought OK, I'm not going to let idiots like Ryan Colby make me feel bad any more. I was so nervous **(58)** .... I chose the wrong music on my MP3 player. So instead of Mozart I was listening to my dance collection.

The problem is that when I have dance music on the headphones I can't stop myself talking **(59)** .... the same rhythm as the music. Most people in school have never heard me speak. They weren't expecting a rap about bacteria that eat plastic. When I finished they all stood up and cheered; suddenly everyone in school wanted to be my friend. They didn't know **(60)** .... my trick with the music, so they just thought I was a brilliant rapper, ha ha!

EXTRA SECTION 2

GRAMMAR KNOWLEDGE

A1/A2 Task 1

Read carefully and answer the following questions (**1-10**).

---

1. Complete the following sentence with the correct form of the verbs in brackets: present perfect or past simple?

Sarah is angry with Leonard. He ____________ (*to fail*) the Biology exam again and he also ____________ (*to fail*) the History exam last month.

---

2. Complete the space in the following sentence appropriately: 'Mr Bianco is a ________ charming man.'

A. ☐ very much
B. ☐ lot
C. ☐ very
D. ☐ too

---

3. Complete the following sentences, by deleting the wrong option appropriately.

a) Don't worry. I *won't forget/am not forgetting* to buy some bread on my way back home.
b) It's freezing today! It *will/is going to* snow later.
c) Do they know what *is happening/will happen* to that music contest in the future?

---

4. Complete the space in the following sentence appropriately: 'Mark, there's a blue pen on the desk ___________ to the television; can you pass it to me, please?'

A. ☐ next
B. ☐ beside
C. ☐ after
D. ☐ before

---

5. Complete the space in the following sentence appropriately: 'If you finish work early, ____________________ and see me at home.'

A. ☐ come around
B. ☐ come on
C. ☐ pass through
D. ☐ take off

6. Complete the space in the following sentence appropriately: 'Her beloved cat died suddenly, but Margaret will ____________ it in time.'

A. ☐ go on
B. ☐ get over
C. ☐ give up
D. ☐ be against

---

7. Complete the space in the following sentence appropriately: 'Sasha always ____________ her bed before going to school.'

A. ☐ makes
B. ☐ does
C. ☐ made
D. ☐ none of the other answers provided is correct

---

8. Complete the space in the following sentence appropriately: 'Lisa, can you go ____________ and fetch me a sweater? I'm a bit cold.'

A. ☐ along
B. ☐ through
C. ☐ towards
D. ☐ upstairs

---

9. Complete the space in the following sentence appropriately: 'Paul doesn't watch TV. He doesn't read magazines ____________.'

A. ☐ too
B. ☐ either
C. ☐ neither
D. ☐ never

---

10. Complete the space in the following sentence appropriately: 'Bill reads a book for about three hours ________________ .'

A. ☐ every evening
B. ☐ all evening
C. ☐ every evenings
D. ☐ all evenings

A1/A2 Task 2

Read carefully and answer the following questions (**11-20**).

11. Complete the following sentences, by deleting the wrong option appropriately.

a) There aren't *any/no* pictures on your sister's bedroom walls.
b) 'How much luggage have you got, Sarah?' '*None/Any*'.
c) The weather was cold, but there was *no/none* wind.

12. Complete the space in the following sentence appropriately: 'My new lamp doesn't work. I am going to ______________ to the shop.'

A. ☐ take it back
B. ☐ turn it on
C. ☐ bring it
D. ☐ pick it up

13. Complete the space in the following sentence appropriately: 'Wait a minute, Jack! Don't go ___________ because I want to ask you something.'

A. ☐ back
B. ☐ away
C. ☐ down
D. ☐ on

14. Complete the space in the following sentence appropriately: 'Why are you so tired? Did you ___________ to bed late last night?'

A. ☐ go
B. ☐ been
C. ☐ went
D. ☐ were

15. Complete the space in the following sentence appropriately: '______________. Can you close that window over there, please?'

A. ☐ It has cold
B. ☐ I'm cold
C. ☐ I cold
D. ☐ I have cold

16. Complete the space in the following sentence appropriately: 'Tommy has been in Canada ________________ now.'

A. ☐ six months ago
B. ☐ for six months
C. ☐ since six months
D. ☐ in six months

---

17. Complete the space in the following sentence appropriately: 'That hospital over there ________________ more than 100 years ago.'

A. ☐ is built
B. ☐ was built
C. ☐ built
D. ☐ was building

---

18. Complete the space in the following sentence appropriately: 'It ________________, so we didn't need an umbrella.'

A. ☐ wasn't rain
B. ☐ wasn't raining
C. ☐ didn't raining
D. ☐ wasn't rained

---

19. Complete the space in the following sentence appropriately: 'I am having a party on the 23rd of May, but Richard and Ingrid ________________ .'

A. ☐ can't come
B. ☐ couldn't come
C. ☐ can't coming
D. ☐ can't to come

---

20. Which of the following sentences is incorrect?

A. ☐ Shall we meet us at 9 am?
B. ☐ Why don't we meet at 9 am?
C. ☐ Shall we meet up at 9 am?
D. ☐ How about meeting at 9 am?

A1/A2 Task 3

Read carefully and answer the following questions (**21-30**).

21. Complete the space in the following sentence appropriately: 'When did Alice go out?' '________________________.'

A. ☐ For twenty minutes
B. ☐ Since twenty minutes
C. ☐ In twenty minutes
D. ☐ Twenty minutes ago

22. Complete the space in the following sentence appropriately: '____________________ to the cinema on Sunday evening. Do you want to come with us?'

A. ☐ We go
B. ☐ We will go
C. ☐ We are going
D. ☐ We will going

23. Complete the space in the following sentence appropriately: 'There's a good film on TV tonight. ________________________ it.'

A. ☐ I watch
B. ☐ I'll watch
C. ☐ I'm going to watch
D. ☐ I'll watching

24. Complete the space in the following sentence appropriately: 'You haven't met my mother yet, ____________________?'

A. ☐ have you
B. ☐ did you
C. ☐ haven't you
D. ☐ do you

25. Complete the space in the following sentence appropriately: 'Excuse me, ____________________ a hotel near here?'

A. ☐ there is
B. ☐ is there
C. ☐ is it
D. ☐ has there

26. Complete the space in the following sentence appropriately: 'When ______________________________?' 'I am not sure... More than 100 years ago.'

A. ☐ was the telephone invented
B. ☐ has the telephone invented
C. ☐ was invented the telephone
D. ☐ did the telephone invented

27. Complete the following sentence with the correct form of the verb in brackets.

Mark, you can turn off the television. I ____________________ (*not/to watch*) it anymore!

28. Complete the following sentences, by deleting the wrong option appropriately.

a) Sometimes we *are going/go* away for the weekend.
b) '*Are you speaking/Do you speak* Chinese?' 'Yes, a little.'
c) Simona is in her office now. She *is talking/talks* with somebody.

29. Consider the following sentences:

a) Don't forget to turn off the light when you go out.
b) Enjoy your trip, and don't forget to send me a postcard!
c) I like this room, but I don't like colour of the carpet.

Which of them is/are incorrect?

A. ☐ a, b, c
B. ☐ a, c
C. ☐ c
D. ☐ a, b

30. Complete the space in the following sentence appropriately: 'A lot of people ____________ television every day.'

A. ☐ watch
B. ☐ watches
C. ☐ look
D. ☐ looks

A1/A2 Task 4

Read carefully and answer the following questions (**31-40**).

31. Complete the spaces in the following sentence appropriately: 'I don't usually buy ___________ in the morning, but I ___________ this morning. There was an interesting story in it!'

A. ☐ a paper; did
B. ☐ a paper; have done
C. ☐ some paper; did
D. ☐ paper; did

32. Complete the space in the following sentence appropriately: 'Jake is really happy: he's got _________________ in a multi-national company. It's such a big change from his old one…'

A. ☐ a new job
B. ☐ new job
C. ☐ a new work
D. ☐ new work

33. Complete the following sentence, by deleting the wrong options appropriately.

'When Eva White *was/has been* younger she wanted to be *a/an* musician; now many people think she's *a/the* best trumpet player in the world.'

34. Complete the following sentences, by deleting the wrong option appropriately.

a) I *know/have known* my husband, Samuel, since I was ten years old.
b) Excuse me, where is the *most near/nearest* bookshop?
c) Bangkok is *a/the* capital of Thailand.

35. Complete the space in the following sentence appropriately: 'This restaurant looks very busy… Is there ____________________?'

A. ☐ anywhere to sit
B. ☐ nowhere to sit
C. ☐ anything to sit
D. ☐ something to sit

36. Complete the space in the following sentence appropriately: 'I saw Tiziana at the airport when I was going to work this morning but she __________ me.'

A. ☐ don't see
B. ☐ didn't see
C. ☐ hasn't seen
D. ☐ didn't saw

---

37. Consider the following sentences:

a) My brother want to be a teacher when he finishes college.
b) We had a dog, but he died last year.
c) Do we have to live know? I'm enjoying myself so much!

Which of them is/are incorrect?

A. ☐ a, c
B. ☐ a, b, c
C. ☐ a only
D. ☐ a, b

---

38. Complete the space in the following sentence appropriately: 'What do you hope __________ when you finish studying?'

A. ☐ to do
B. ☐ do
C. ☐ doing
D. ☐ done

---

39. Complete the space in the following sentence appropriately: 'You didn't need __________ any more eggs. We had some in the fridge.'

A. ☐ buy
B. ☐ buying
C. ☐ to buy
D. ☐ having bought

---

40. Complete the space in the following sentence appropriately: 'Johannes, please don't forget to text me when you __________ home!'

A. ☐ get
B. ☐ are getting
C. ☐ are going to get
D. ☐ will get

1 Il plurale dei nomi

- Il **plurale dei nomi** si ottiene aggiungendo **-s** al nome singolare: *book* → *books*.
  - Se il nome singolare termina in **-s**, **-ss**, **-sh**, **-ch**, **-x**, **-o**, **-z**, si aggiunge **-es**: *bus* → *buses*.
  - Alcuni nomi terminanti in **-o**, tuttavia, aggiungono solo la **-s**: *discos*, *photos*, *pianos*, *videos*, *radios*.
  - Se il nome singolare termina con consonante + **-y**, si toglie la **-y** e si aggiunge **-ies**: *country* → *countries*.
  - Se il nome singolare termina con **-f** o **-fe**, questi si tolgono e si aggiunge **-ves**: *shelf* → *shelves*; *life* → *lives*.
- Alcuni plurali sono irregolari:

child → *children*	*man* → *men*
tooth → *teeth*	*person* → *people*
woman → *women*	*foot* → *feet*
mouse → *mice*	

- In alcuni casi invece il plurale è uguale al singolare:

one fish → *two fish*	*one sheep* → *two sheep*

2 Le *question words*

- Le ***question words*** si usano per formulare domande. Si collocano sempre all'inizio della frase interrogativa.
  Who is your English teacher? = Chi è il tuo / vostro insegnante di inglese?
  What's your name? = Qual è il tuo nome? / Come ti chiami?
  When is your birthday? = Quand'è il tuo compleanno?
  How are you? = Come stai?
  How old are you? = Quanti anni hai?
- Le eventuali preposizioni vanno alla fine della frase:
  *Where are you **from**?* = Di dove sei?
- ***What*** e ***which*** significano entrambi "quale", ma ***which*** si usa per indicare **una scelta tra due o più opzioni**:
  What are your favourite books? = Quali sono i tuoi libri preferiti?
  Which is your first language, English or Italian? = Qual è la tua prima lingua, l'inglese o l'italiano?

3 Il genitivo sassone e *whose*

- In inglese il possesso o il rapporto tra persone si esprime con il nome del **possessore** + ***'s*** + **nome della cosa** o della persona, senza l'articolo:
  It's Sue's birthday. = È il compleanno di Sue.
  She's Becky's mum. = È la mamma di Becky.
- Quando due persone possiedono qualcosa insieme si aggiunge ***'s*** alla seconda persona:
  This is Alex and Jamie's room. = Questa è la stanza di Alex e Jamie.
- Ai nomi che terminano in **-s** e ai plurali regolari si aggiunge solo l'apostrofo:
  Clara is Janis' cousin. = Clara è la cugina di Janis.
  This is the girls' room. = Questa è la camera delle ragazze.

Attenzione !
La s preceduta dall'apostrofo ('s) può essere:
- ***is***, terza persona singolare di *be*: *Anne's happy.* = Anne è felice.
- ***has***, terza persona singolare di *have got*: *Anne's got two sisters.* = Anne ha due sorelle.
- la ***'s*** che esprime possesso: *This is Anne's mobile phone.* = Questo è il cellulare di Anne.

- ***Whose*** significa "Di chi?" ed è usato come aggettivo o come pronome. Si possono avere due costruzioni:
  Whose pen is it? oppure *Whose is this pen?* = Di chi è questa penna?

4 *Present simple*

- Il ***Present simple*** si ottiene con la forma base del verbo, cioè la forma che trovi sul dizionario (infinito senza *to*). Alla terza persona singolare (*he* / *she* / *it*) si aggiunge **-s** alla forma base.
- Il ***Present simple*** si usa per parlare di azioni abituali, di attività frequenti, di situazioni permanenti e di fatti che sono sempre veri:
  I get up at 7 o'clock. = Mi alzo alle sette in punto.
  They live in Spain. = Vivono in Spagna.
  Water boils at 100°C. = L'acqua bolle a 100°C.
- La **forma negativa** si ottiene con: **soggetto** + ***do*** / ***does*** + ***not*** + **forma base** (forma estesa) o **soggetto** + ***don't*** / ***doesn't*** + **forma base** (forma contratta). La forma contratta è la più usata nell'inglese parlato e in quello scritto informale:
  Terry doesn't play volleyball. = Terry non gioca a pallavolo.
- La struttura delle **frasi interrogative** è: ***do*** / ***does*** + **soggetto** + **forma base del verbo** + **?**

- La struttura delle **risposte brevi** è: ***Yes***, + **pronome soggetto** + ***do*** / ***does***; ***No***, + **pronome soggetto** + ***don't*** / ***doesn't***:
'Do they watch TV at night?' 'No, they don't.' = "Guardano la TV di sera?" "No."

-ch, -sh, -ss, -x, -zz, -o	*-es*
watch	watch**es**
wash	wash**es**
kiss	kiss**es**
relax	relax**es**
buzz	buzz**es**
do	do**es**

consonante + *-y*	*-ies*
study	stud**ies**
vocale + *-y*	***-s***
play	play**s**

Attenzione !
Il verbo ***do*** viene usato sia come ausiliare per ottenere la forma negativa, interrogativa e le risposte brevi del *Present simple*, sia come un normale verbo che significa "fare":
I do sport every day. = Faccio sport tutti i giorni.
Jenny doesn't do sport. = Jenny non fa sport.
Do you do sport every day? = Fai / Fate sport tutti i giorni?

5 *like, love, hate + -ing*

- In inglese il verbo ***like***, (piacere), ha una costruzione particolare, diversa da quella italiana: **soggetto** (la persona a cui piace qualcosa) + ***like*** + **oggetto** (ciò che piace):
I like pizza. = Mi piace la pizza.
Jeff doesn't like musicals. = A Jeff non piacciono i musical.
- I verbi ***like*** (piacere), ***love*** (amare), ***hate*** (odiare), ***enjoy*** (divertirsi, godersi qualcosa) sono seguiti dalla forma in ***-ing*** del verbo:
I like playing tennis. = Mi piace giocare a tennis.
They hate cleaning their room. = Odiano pulire la loro stanza.

Forma base	Forma in *-ing*
eat	eat**ing**
pla**y**	play**ing**
stud**y**	study**ing**
hav**e**	hav**ing**
sto**p**	stop**ping**
l**ie**	l**ying**

6 I nomi numerabili e non numerabili

- Sono numerabili (***countable***) i nomi di cose, animali e persone che si possono contare e che hanno forma plurale: *eggs*, *biscuits*, *oranges*, ecc.
- Sono non numerabili (***uncountable***) i nomi di cose che non si possono contare e che hanno solo la forma singolare: *sugar*, *water*, *bread*, ecc.
- Non si può mai usare l'articolo indeterminativo (*a* / *an*) davanti ai sostantivi non numerabili. Per indicare una quantità precisa con i sostantivi non numerabili bisogna usare altre espressioni:
  - *a glass of water* = un bicchiere d'acqua
  - *a packet of sugar* = un pacchetto di zucchero
  - *a piece* / *a slice of bread* = un pezzo / una fetta di pane
  - *a cup of coffee* / *tea* = una tazza di caffè / tè
  - *a bottle of water* / *milk* = una bottiglia d'acqua / di latte

7 Gli avverbi di frequenza

- Si usano per indicare con quale frequenza viene compiuta un'azione. L'avverbio di frequenza segue il verbo *be*, ma precede gli altri verbi:
You are always late for school. = Sei sempre in ritardo per la scuola.
We often go to the cinema. = Andiamo spesso al cinema.

8 *some / any*

- Si usano ***some*** e ***any*** per indicare una quantità non definita, sia con nomi numerabili plurali (libri, biscotti, amici) sia con nomi non numerabili (latte, pasta, caffè). Corrispondono all'italiano "un po', alcuni, qualche, del, della, dei, degli, delle".
- Nelle frasi affermative si usa ***some***:
There is some milk. = C'è del latte.
I've got some comics. = Ho dei fumetti.
- Nelle frasi negative e nelle domande si usa ***any***:
She hasn't got any dolls. = Non ha bambole.
Is there any dessert? = C'è del dolce?

9 *How much? / How many?*

- ***How much*** e ***How many*** si usano per informarsi sulla quantità di qualcosa.
- ***How much*** (quanto, quanta) si usa con i sostantivi non numerabili e per chiedere il prezzo di qualcosa:
  How much ice cream is there? = Quanto gelato c'è?
  How much are the pizzas? = Quanto costano / vengono le pizze?
- ***How many*** (quanti, quante) si usa con i sostantivi numerabili plurali:
  How many posters have you got in your room? = Quanti poster hai nella tua stanza / in camera tua?

10 Il verbo modale *can / can't*

- Il verbo ***can*** significa potere, saper (fare), riuscire, e si usa, tra le altre cose, per esprimere l'abilità, la capacità di fare qualcosa. È un verbo modale ed è uguale per tutte le persone.
  È sempre seguito dalla forma base del verbo principale:
  I can sing. = So cantare.
- Per la **forma negativa** si aggiunge ***not***:
  I can't play the guitar. = Non so suonare la chitarra.
- La struttura delle **frasi interrogative** è: ***Can*** + **soggetto** + **forma base del verbo**.
- La struttura delle **risposte brevi** è: ***Yes,*** + **pronome soggetto** + ***can.*** / ***No,*** + **pronome soggetto** + ***can't***:
  'Can you speak French?' 'Yes, I can.' / 'No, I can't.' = "Parli / Sai parlare il francese?" "Sì." / "No."

11 *Present continuous*

- Il ***Present continuous*** si usa per indicare azioni che si stanno svolgendo nel momento in cui si parla, o per due azioni che si svolgono contemporaneamente.
- È spesso accompagnato da espressioni di tempo come ***now*** (adesso, ora), ***at the moment*** (in questo momento), ***today*** (oggi).
- La **forma affermativa** si ottiene con: **soggetto** + ***am*** / ***are*** / ***is*** + **forma in *-ing*** del verbo:
  I am wearing jeans at the moment. = Sto indossando / Indosso i jeans in questo momento.
  It's raining today. = Oggi piove.
- La **forma negativa** si ottiene con: **soggetto** + ***am*** / ***are*** / ***is*** + ***not*** + **forma in *-ing*** del verbo:
  It isn't snowing at the moment. = Non nevica in questo momento.
- La **forma interrogativa** si ottiene con: ***am*** / ***are*** / ***is*** + **soggetto** + **forma in *-ing*** del verbo + **?**
- Le **risposte brevi** sono identiche alle risposte brevi del presente di *be*:
  'Are they doing their homework?' 'Yes, they are.' / 'No, they aren't.' = "Fanno / Stanno facendo i compiti?" "Sì." "No."

In italiano il *Present continuous* si traduce con il verbo "stare" seguito dal gerundio, ma anche con il presente indicativo.

- Il *Present continuous* NON si usa con i seguenti verbi: *hear, see, love, like, want, believe, know*.

12 Il *Past simple* di *be* + espressioni di tempo passato

- Il ***Past simple*** di *be* ha due voci: ***was*** per la prima e la terza persona singolari, ***were*** per la seconda persona singolare e per le persone plurali. In italiano può corrispondere al passato remoto, al passato prossimo oppure all'imperfetto. Si usa per indicare azioni o situazioni accadute in un determinato tempo del passato e concluse.
- Spesso è accompagnato da **espressioni di tempo al passato** come *yesterday, last night / week / month / year, a month / year / three days ago, in 1955, when I was a child…*
  We were at the seaside last month. = Eravamo al mare il mese scorso.
  This house was built in 1980. = Questa casa è stata costruita nel 1980.
  They were here a month ago. = Erano qui un mese fa.
- Le **forme negativa** e **interrogativa** e le **risposte brevi** seguono le stesse regole di formazione del verbo *be* al *Present simple*:
  Where were you yesterday morning? = Dov'eri ieri mattina?
  'Was she blonde when she was a child?' 'Yes, she was!' = "Era bionda da bambina?" "Sì!"

13 *Past simple*

- Il ***Past simple*** si usa per parlare di azioni ed eventi completamente conclusi nel passato. Il ***Past simple*** dei verbi regolari si ottiene aggiungendo ***-ed*** alla forma base del verbo ed è uguale per tutte le persone. Alcuni verbi subiscono delle variazioni ortografiche.
  I played volleyball yesterday. = Ieri ho giocato a pallavolo.
- I **verbi irregolari** non aggiungono ***-ed*** ma hanno una forma propria che va imparata a memoria (vedi la tabella a pag. 208). Anche per i verbi irregolari il ***Past simple*** è uguale per tutte le persone, fatta eccezione per il verbo ***be***.
  They ate a lot last night. = Hanno mangiato molto ieri sera.
- Per le **forme interrogativa** e **negativa** e per le **risposte brevi** si deve usare l'ausiliare ***did*** / ***didn't***.

> **Attenzione !**
> Ricorda che in presenza di un ausiliare il verbo principale resta sempre alla forma base!

She didn't play basketball three years ago. = Non giocava a basket tre anni fa.
Did your sister like the present? = A tua sorella è piaciuto il regalo?
Yes, she did. / No, she didn't. = Sì. / No.
What did you do yesterday afternoon? = Cosa hai fatto ieri pomeriggio?

14 Il verbo modale *could / couldn't*

- ***Could*** è il passato e il condizionale di ***can*** e si usa per:
  - indicare abilità o inabilità nel passato:
    They couldn't book a table at the restaurant. = Non riuscirono a prenotare un tavolo al ristorante.
  - indicare la possibilità o l'impossibilità di fare qualcosa al passato:
    I couldn't call you yesterday. My phone wasn't working. = Non ti ho potuto chiamare ieri. Il mio telefono non funzionava.
  - fare una richiesta in modo formale e cortese:
    Could you repeat the instructions, please? = Può ripetere le istruzioni, per piacere?
  - esprimere un suggerimento:
    You could do more exercise. = Potresti fare più movimento.

15 I pronomi relativi *who, which, that*

- ***Who***, ***which*** e ***that*** sono pronomi relativi (***relative pronouns***) che mettono in relazione due proposizioni, quella reggente e quella subordinata relativa, in cui vengono aggiunte ulteriori informazioni su un sostantivo o un pronome nominato nella reggente.
- Sono invariabili in genere e numero: ***who*** (oppure ***that***) si usa per le persone; ***which*** (oppure ***that***) si usa per animali e oggetti.
- Quando il pronome relativo è il **soggetto** della frase relativa **deve sempre essere espresso**. Quando il pronome relativo è complemento oggetto può essere omesso:
  *The boy **who / that** is talking to Nick is my friend.* = Il ragazzo **che** sta parlando con Nick è un mio amico. (soggetto)
  *This is the film **which / that** won a special award in 2016.* = Questo è il film **che** ha vinto un premio speciale nel 2016. (soggetto)
  *She's the girl (**who / that**) I met at Leo's party.* = È la ragazza che ho incontrato alla festa di Leo. (oggetto)
  *Show me the photos (**which / that**) you took in Paris.* = Fammi vedere le foto che hai fatto a Parigi. (oggetto)

A differenza dell'inglese, in italiano questi pronomi relativi possono essere espressi da "che" (invariabile in genere e numero) oppure da "il quale, la quale, i quali, le quali" che invece si accordano in genere e numero. Non c'è differenza tra persone, animali e oggetti.

16 Il comparativo degli aggettivi

- Per confrontare due persone, cose o categorie si usa il comparativo di un aggettivo + ***than*** che introduce il secondo termine di paragone.
- Gli aggettivi brevi aggiungono ***-er***:
  Colin is shorter than his brother. = Colin è più basso di suo fratello.
- Osserva le variazioni ortografiche:
  - se l'aggettivo termina con **una vocale** + **una consonante** si raddoppia la consonante:
    fat → *fatter*
  - se termina per ***-e*** muta si aggiunge soltanto ***-r***:
    large → *larger*
  - se termina in ***-y*** preceduta da consonante si toglie la ***-y*** e si aggiunge ***-ier***: *easy* → *easier*

- Gli aggettivi lunghi sono preceduti da ***more***:
Maths tests are more difficult than English tests. = Le verifiche di matematica sono più difficili di quelle di inglese.

Attenzione !
Alcuni comparativi sono irregolari:
good / well → better; bad → worse; far → further / farther.

17 Il superlativo degli aggettivi

- Si usa il **superlativo relativo** di un aggettivo per paragonare una cosa o persona con tutte le altre cose o persone in quel gruppo. Gli aggettivi brevi aggiungono ***-est***:
Jamie is the shortest in his class. = Jamie è il più basso della classe.

- Osserva le variazioni ortografiche:
  - se l'aggettivo termina con **una vocale** + **una consonante** si raddoppia la consonante:
  *fat → the fat**test***
  - se termina per ***-e*** muta si aggiunge soltanto ***-st***:
  *large → the large**st***
  - se termina in ***-y*** preceduta da consonante si toglie la ***-y*** e si aggiunge ***-iest***: *easy → the eas**iest***.

- Gli aggettivi lunghi sono preceduti da ***the most***:
Chemistry tests are the most difficult. = Le verifiche di chimica sono le più difficili.

Attenzione !
Alcuni superlativi sono irregolari:
good / well → the best; bad → the worst; far → the furthest / farthest.

- L'aggettivo al grado superlativo è sempre preceduto dall'articolo ***the*** e può essere seguito da ***in*** + **luogo** o gruppo di persone oppure da ***of*** + **nome** o pronome plurale.

18 Il comparativo di uguaglianza: *(not) as ... as*

- Il comparativo di uguaglianza si forma con (***not***) ***as*** + **aggettivo** + ***as***. Si usa per dire che due cose, animali o persone hanno o non hanno la stessa qualità:
I'm as tall as my sister. = Sono alto quanto mia sorella.

19 *have to / don't have to*

- Si usa ***have to*** + **forma base** del verbo per esprimere un dovere o un obbligo imposto da qualcun altro. ***Have to*** non è un verbo modale, ha tutti i tempi e i modi e si usa anche per coniugare ***must***, "dovere", nei tempi mancanti. Il verbo ***have to*** costruisce le forme negativa e interrogativa e le risposte brevi con l'ausiliare ***do***:
You have to wear a uniform in this school. = Dovete indossare la divisa in questa scuola.
'Did you have to wear a uniform at primary school?' 'Yes, I did./ No, I didn't.' = "Dovevi indossare una divisa alle scuole elementari?" "Sì. / No."

Attenzione !
La **forma negativa** (***don't have to*** + forma base del verbo) si usa per indicare che non è necessario o non è obbligatorio fare qualcosa:
I don't have to go to school on Sundays. = Non devo andare a scuola di sabato.

20 *must / mustn't*

- Il verbo ***must*** è un verbo modale, perciò è uguale per tutte le persone, è sempre seguito dalla forma base del verbo principale e usa solo ***not*** (***n't***) per la forma negativa. Si usa ***must*** per dare un ordine o esprimere un dovere, un obbligo, spesso avvertito dal soggetto stesso:
I can't come with you. I must study. = Non posso venire con te. Devo studiare.

- Si usa ***mustn't*** per esprimere una proibizione o un divieto:
You mustn't run in the corridor. = Non dovete correre nel corridoio.

Attenzione !
Must e ***mustn't*** si usano soltanto al presente. Per costruire i tempi mancanti del verbo "dovere" si usa ***have to***.

21 *be going to*

- Il futuro con ***be going to*** si ottiene con il presente del verbo *be* seguito da *going to* e dalla forma base del verbo principale. Si usa:
  - per esprimere l'intenzione di fare qualcosa nel futuro:
  She's going to have a party next week. = Darà / Ha intenzione di dare una festa la settimana prossima.
  What are you going to do after the university? = Che farai dopo l'università?

- per fare previsioni sulla base di ciò che vediamo o per indicare un evento che sta per accadere:
  Look at the sky. It's going to snow. = Guarda il cielo. Sta per nevicare. / Nevicherà.

22 Past participle

- Il ***Past participle*** dei verbi regolari segue le stesse regole di formazione del *Past simple*: si aggiunge ***-ed*** alla forma base del verbo. Il ***Past participle*** dei verbi irregolari varia. (vedi pag. 208)

23 Present perfect

- Il ***Present perfect*** si forma con **soggetto** + ***have*** / ***has*** + ***Past participle*** del verbo principale. Per la forma negativa si aggiunge ***not*** dopo il verbo ausiliare. Nella forma interrogativa il verbo ausiliare precede il soggetto.
- Il ***Present perfect*** si usa per parlare di azioni avvenute in un tempo non precisato del passato: l'attenzione è posta sull'azione e i suoi effetti sul presente, non su quando è avvenuta:
  The film has ended. = Il film è finito.
  The teacher hasn't given any homework. = L'insegnante non ha dato compiti.
  Have you seen my sweatshirt? = Hai visto la mia felpa?
- Si usa anche per indicare azioni avvenute in un passato recente oppure in un periodo di tempo non ancora concluso. In questi casi è spesso accompagnato da espressioni di tempo come *recently, today, this morning / week / month / year…* che di solito si trovano alla fine della frase:
  I haven't heard the news today. = Non ho sentito le notizie oggi.

Attenzione !
Come participio passato di ***go*** si usa ***gone*** per indicare che qualcuno è andato in un luogo e non è ancora tornato, ***been*** per indicare che quella persona è stata in un luogo ed è tornata:
Lisa has gone to the gym. = Lisa è andata in palestra. (non è ancora tornata)
Lisa has been to the gym. = Lisa è andata / stata in palestra. (è tornata)

24 Present perfect with ever and never

- Gli avverbi ***ever*** (nelle frasi interrogative) e ***never*** (nelle frasi negative, lasciando il verbo affermativo) si usano con il ***Present perfect*** per parlare di azioni mai fatte prima:
  Have you ever listened to classical music? = Hai mai ascoltato musica classica?
  They've never studied Russian. = Non hanno mai studiato il russo.

Ricorda !
Questi avverbi si trovano sempre prima del participio passato.

25 Present perfect with for, since and how long

- Il ***Present perfect*** si usa anche per descrivere un'azione iniziata nel passato e che continua nel presente (forma di durata).
- Per indicare il **momento iniziale** dell'azione si usa ***since***:
  She has lived in this house since she was a child / 2015 / last summer. = Vive in questa casa da quando era bambina / dal 2015 / dall'estate scorsa.
- Per indicare la **durata** dell'azione si usa ***for***:
  I've been here for an hour/ three years / a long time. = Sono qui da un'ora / tre anni / tanto tempo.
- Per chiedere **da quanto tempo** è iniziata un'azione si usa ***How long***. ***How long*** può significare "da quando" oppure "da quanto tempo":
  How long have you been here? = Da quando / Da quanto tempo sei qui?

In italiano la forma di durata si traduce con il **presente indicativo**. Sia ***for*** che ***since*** significano "da".

26 Present perfect or Past simple?

- Si usa il ***Past simple*** per parlare di azioni ed eventi conclusi in un tempo determinato del passato o che non hanno nessun legame con il presente.
  È accompagnato da espressioni di tempo come ***yesterday***, ***two days ago***, ***last month*** / ***year***. Per la formazione, ricorda che i verbi possono essere regolari e irregolari. (Per la lista dei verbi irregolari, vai alla pagina 208.)

- Per le **forme negativa** e **interrogativa** usiamo l'ausiliare ***did*** seguito dalla forma base del verbo principale:
  I saw her yesterday. = L'ho vista ieri.
  When did you see her? = Quando l'hai vista?
  I didn't see her yesterday. = Non l'ho vista ieri.
- Si usa il ***Present perfect*** per parlare di azioni terminate da poco e per esprimere il risultato presente di un'azione passata (con ***just***, ***already***, ***yet***):
  *I've **just** seen her.* = L'ho appena vista.
- Si usa anche per descrivere avvenimenti ed esperienze senza un riferimento preciso di tempo o che non sono mai avvenuti (con ***ever*** e ***never***).
  I've never run a marathon! = Non ho mai corso una maratona!
- Si usa inoltre per azioni avvenute in un tempo passato non ancora concluso:
  I've read five books this month. = Ho letto cinque libri questo mese.
- Anche la **forma di durata** si esprime con il ***Present perfect***, accompagnato da ***for*** e ***since*** e dalle domande con ***How long...?***:
  They've lived in France for ten years. = Vivono in Francia da dieci anni.
- Ricorda che anche il participio passato dei verbi irregolari cambia (vedi pag. 208)

27 Il futuro con *will*

- Il futuro con ***will*** (***Future simple***) si usa per fare previsioni sul futuro, per fare promesse e con i verbi di opinione ***think***, ***know***, ***believe***, ***hope***:
  I promise I'll come to your party. = Prometto che verrò alla tua festa.
  We think we'll go to the cinema on Saturday. = Pensiamo di andare al cinema sabato.
- La **forma affermativa** e quella **negativa** si ottengono con **soggetto** + ***will*** (***'ll***) / ***will not*** (***won't***) + **forma base** del verbo:
  It won't snow a lot this winter. = Non nevicherà molto questo inverno.
- La **forma interrogativa** si ottiene con ***will*** + **soggetto** + **forma base** del verbo + ...?:
  Will they reply to my request? = Risponderanno alla mia richiesta?
- Per la prima persona singolare e plurale si può usare anche l'ausiliare ***shall***, ma nell'inglese parlato e informale si usa ***will*** per tutte le persone, di solito alla forma contratta ***'ll***.

28 *be going to o will?*

- Si usa il futuro con ***be going to*** seguito dalla forma base del verbo principale per esprimere l'intenzione di fare qualcosa:
  I'm going to study abroad. = Studierò / Ho intenzione di studiare all'estero.
- Si usa ***be going to*** anche per indicare qualcosa che sta per succedere:
  Look at those clouds. It's going to rain. = Guarda quelle nubi. Sta per piovere. / Pioverà.
- Si usa il futuro con ***will*** / ***won't*** seguito dal verbo principale per parlare di previsioni future, per esprimere un'opinione e per fare promesse:
  The future of the planet will depend on our choices. = Il futuro del pianeta dipenderà dalle nostre scelte.
  I think they will sell the house. = Penso che venderanno la casa.
  I'll come to the match. = Verrò alla partita.
- ***will*** / ***won't*** si usa inoltre nel periodo ipotetico di tipo 1:
  We'll stay at home if it rains. = Resteremo a casa se pioverà.

29 *Zero conditional*

- Lo ***Zero conditional***, o periodo ipotetico generale, si usa per regole generali o leggi scientifiche. Ha due parti: la proposizione principale (***main clause***) che esprime la conseguenza e quella subordinata, introdotta da ***if*** o ***when***, che esprime l'ipotesi. La proposizione subordinata può precedere o seguire quella principale. Il tempo verbale è il ***Present simple*** sia nella ***if clause*** che nella ***main clause***:
  If *you touch a fire, you get burned.* = Se tocchi il fuoco, ti bruci.
  *Ice melts **when** you heat it.* = Il ghiaccio si scioglie quando lo scaldi.
- Lo ***Zero conditional*** si usa anche per dare consigli o comandi; in questo caso nella *main clause* si usa l'imperativo:
  If you drink, don't drive! = Se bevi, non guidare!

30 *First conditional*

- Il ***First conditional*** (periodo ipotetico di tipo 1) indica la **possibilità** o la **probabilità** che una situazione si verifichi nel futuro e si usa per predire possibili azioni o conseguenze future e per dare consigli:
*Will they come to our party **if** we invite them?* = Verranno alla nostra festa se li inviteremo?
***When** I have time, I'll cut the grass.* = Quando avrò tempo taglierò l'erba.

In inglese il verbo della proposizione principale è sempre al futuro con *will*, mentre quello della subordinata è sempre al *Present simple*. In italiano invece il verbo della proposizione subordinata può essere sia al presente indicativo, sia al futuro (doppio futuro).

31 *Second conditional*

- Usiamo il ***Second conditional*** per parlare di situazioni improbabili o immaginarie. La frase subordinata è introdotta da ***if***, mentre il tempo verbale è al *Past simple*; nella frase principale si usa ***would*** (***'d***), seguito dalla forma base del verbo:
***If** I read that book, I **would** know the answer.* = Se avessi letto quel libro, saprei la risposta.

32 *may e might*

- ***May*** e ***might*** si usano per esprimere una possibilità presente o futura e per fare previsioni:
The weather forecast says it may/might snow tomorrow. = Le previsioni del tempo dicono che potrebbe nevicare domani.
- La **forma affermativa** si ottiene con **soggetto** + ***may***/***might*** + **forma base** del verbo: *Kath may/might join us later.* = Kath potrebbe raggiungerci più tardi.
- La **forma negativa** si ottiene con **soggetto** + ***may***/***might not*** + **forma base** del verbo: *Kath may/might not join us.* = Kath potrebbe non raggiungerci.

Attenzione!
Non esiste la forma negativa contratta di *may*.

Le frasi con ***may***/***might*** possono essere tradotte in italiano in diversi modi:
They may/might come later. = Potrebbero arrivare più tardi. / Può darsi che arrivino più tardi. / Forse arriveranno più tardi.

33 Composti di *some, any, no, every*

- Con ***some***, ***any***, ***no*** ed ***every*** si possono costruire pronomi e avverbi indefiniti che si riferiscono alle persone, alle cose e ai luoghi. Gli indefiniti composti sono sempre seguiti da un verbo alla terza persona singolare.
- I composti di ***some*** si usano nelle frasi affermative:
Somebody / Someone is knocking at the door. = Qualcuno sta bussando alla porta.
- I composti di ***any*** si usano nelle frasi negative e nelle domande:
Is there anything to eat? = C'è qualcosa da mangiare?
There isn't anything on TV tonight. = Non c'è niente in TV stasera.

Attenzione!
Se la domanda è un'**offerta** oppure una **richiesta** si usano di solito i composti di ***some***:
Would you like / Can I have something to drink? = Vorresti / Posso avere qualcosa da bere?

- I composti di ***no*** si usano con il verbo alla forma affermativa:
Nobody went to the meeting. = Nessuno andò alla riunione.

34 *Need*

- Il verbo ***need*** significa "aver bisogno di" ed è un verbo regolare. Può essere seguito da un sostantivo o da ***to*** + **forma base** del verbo. È usato per esprimere necessità o mancanza di necessità:
I need a new pair of shoes. = Ho bisogno di un nuovo paio di scarpe.
They don't need to rush. = Non hanno bisogno / Non devono affrettarsi.

Attenzione!
Osserva la differenza:
You don't need to shout. (*need* è verbo) = Non devi / Non è necessario che tu urli.
There's no need to shout. (*need* è sostantivo) = Non c'è bisogno di urlare.

35 Il *Past continuous*

- Il ***Past continuous*** si forma con ***was*** / ***were*** + la forma in ***-ing*** del verbo principale. Le **forme interrogativa** e **negativa** e le **risposte brevi** seguono le regole di formazione del verbo *be* al *Past simple*. Si usa per descrivere azioni che erano in corso di svolgimento in un momento del passato:

In italiano il ***Past continuous*** si può tradurre con **l'imperfetto** oppure con il verbo **stare** + **gerundio**.

What were you doing this morning at 7? = Cosa facevi / stavi facendo alle 7 di questa mattina?
I was sleeping. = Dormivo / Stavo dormendo.

- Il ***Past continuous*** si usa spesso in una frase introdotta da ***while***, "mentre", quando due azioni sono simultanee:
They were talking ***while*** *she was cooking dinner.* = Parlavano mentre lei preparava la cena.

36 *Past continuous* e *Past simple* con *when* e *while*

- Il ***Past continuous*** può anche essere usato per indicare un'azione in corso di svolgimento nel passato che viene interrotta da un'altra, oppure un'azione in corso di svolgimento quando se ne verifica improvvisamente un'altra (al *Past simple*). Le due frasi sono di solito collegate da *while* seguito dal *Past continuous*, o da *when* seguito dal *Past simple*:
I was going to the library ***when*** *I met Susan.* = Stavo andando in biblioteca quando ho incontrato Susan.
While *I was drinking a coffee my mobile rang.* = Mentre bevevo un caffè, ha squillato il cellulare.

37 La forma passiva

- La **forma passiva** si usa quando si vuole mettere maggiormente in risalto l'azione rispetto a chi la compie.
- La forma passiva del ***Present simple*** si costruisce con **soggetto** + ***Present simple*** **del verbo *be*** + **participio passato** del verbo principale:
Royal Theatre tickets ***are sold*** *here.* = I biglietti del *Royal Theatre* sono venduti qui.
- Le forme negativa, interrogativa e le risposte brevi seguono le regole di formazione del verbo ***be***.
- La forma passiva del ***Past simple*** si costruisce con **soggetto** + ***Past simple*** **del verbo *be*** + **participio passato** del verbo principale:
The windows were cleaned yesterday. = Le finestre sono state pulite ieri.
- Le forme negativa, interrogativa e le risposte brevi seguono le regole di formazione del verbo ausiliare *be* al *Past simple*.

Attenzione !
Il **complemento d'agente** è sempre introdotto dalla preposizione ***by***:
The leaves are blown ***by*** *the wind.* = Le foglie sono mosse dal vento.

38 Il discorso diretto e indiretto

- Nel **discorso diretto** (***direct speech***) si riportano le parole esatte che vengono dette con una frase tra virgolette:
Billy says: 'Today it is cold.' = Billy dice: "Oggi fa freddo".
- Il **discorso indiretto** (***reported speech***) si usa invece quando riferiamo quello che qualcuno dice o ha detto:
Billy says (that) today it is cold. = Billy dice che oggi fa freddo.
- Il discorso indiretto è introdotto dai verbi ***say*** o ***tell***:
  - si usa ***say*** quando la persona a cui si parla non è indicata: *Jack says Rome is beautiful.* = Jack dice che Roma è bella.
  - si usa ***tell*** quando la persona a cui si parla è indicata: *Jack tells Brian Rome is beautiful.* = Jack dice a Brian che Roma è bella.
- Quando il verbo che introduce il discorso indiretto è al presente, nel passaggio dal discorso diretto a quello indiretto il tempo verbale non cambia. Negli altri casi i tempi verbali cambiano.
She says: 'I miss my friends'. = Lei disse: "Mi mancano i miei amici".
She says that she misses her friends. = Lei dice che le mancano i suoi amici.
- Nel passaggio da discorso diretto a indiretto anche i pronomi personali, gli aggettivi possessivi, i dimostrativi e le espressioni di tempo cambiano sempre:
*Ann said: '****This*** *is* ***my*** *bag'.* = Ann disse: "Questa è la mia borsa".
Ann said ***that*** *was* ***her*** *bag.* = Ann disse che quella era la sua borsa.

be – Present simple

Forma affermativa		Forma negativa	
Estesa	Contratta	Estesa	Contratta
I am	I'm	I am not	I'm not
you are	you're	you are not	you aren't
he / she / it is	he's / she's / it's	he / she / it is not	he / she / it isn't
we are	we're	we are not	we aren't
you are	you're	you are not	you aren't
they are	they're	they are not	they aren't

Forma interrogativa	Risposte brevi	
	Affermative	Negative
Am I... ?	Yes, you are.	No, you aren't.
Are you... ?	Yes, I am.	No, I'm not.
Is he / she / it... ?	Yes, he / she / it is.	No, he / she / it isn't.
Are we... ?	Yes, we are.	No, we aren't.
Are you... ?	Yes, you are.	No, you aren't.
Are they... ?	Yes, they are.	No, they aren't.

be – Past simple

Forma affermativa	Forma negativa	
	Estesa	Contratta
I was	I was not	I wasn't
you were	you were not	you weren't
he / she / it was	he / she / it was not	he / she / it wasn't
we were	we were not	we weren't
you were	you were not	you weren't
they were	they were not	they weren't

Forma interrogativa	Risposte brevi affermative	Risposte brevi negative
Was I... ?	Yes, you were.	No, you weren't.
Were you... ?	Yes, I was.	No, I wasn't.
Was he... / she... ? / it... ?	Yes, he / she / it was.	No, he / she / it wasn't.
Were we... ?	Yes, we were.	No, we weren't.
Were you... ?	Yes, you were.	No, you weren't.
Were they... ?	Yes, they were.	No, they weren't.

have got – Present simple

Forma affermativa		Forma negativa	
Estesa	Contratta	Estesa	Contratta
I have got	I've got	I have not got	I haven't got
you have got	you've got	you have not got	you haven't got
he / she / it has got	he's / she's / it's got	he / she / it has not got	he / she / it hasn't got
we have got	we've got	we have not got	we haven't got
you have got	you've got	you have not got	you haven't got
they have got	they've got	they have not got	they haven't got

Forma interrogativa	Risposte brevi	
	Affermative	Negative
Have I got…?	Yes, you have.	No, you haven't.
Have you got... ?	Yes, I have.	No, I haven't.
Has he / she / it got... ?	Yes, he / she / it has.	No, he / she / it hasn't.
Have we got... ?	Yes, we have.	No, we haven't.
Have you got... ?	Yes, you have.	No, you haven't.
Have they got... ?	Yes, they have.	No, they haven't.

Present simple

Forma affermativa	Forma negativa – Estesa	Forma negativa – Contratta
I live.	I do not live.	I don't live.
You live.	You do not live.	You don't live.
He / She / It lives.	He / She / It does not live.	He / She / It doesn't live.
We live.	We do not live.	We don't live.
You live.	You do not live.	You don't live.
They live.	They do not live.	They don't live.

Forma interrogativa	Risposte brevi – Affermative	Risposte brevi – Negative
Do I live…?	Yes, you do.	No, you don't.
Do you live…?	Yes, I do.	No, I don't.
Does he / she / it live…?	Yes, he / she / it does.	No, he / she / it doesn't.
Do we live…?	Yes, we do.	No, we don't.
Do you live…?	Yes, you do.	No, you don't.
Do they live…?	Yes, they do.	No, they don't.

Present continuous

Forma affermativa	Forma negativa – Estesa	Forma negativa – Contratta
I am walking.	I am not walking.	I'm not walking.
You are walking	You are not walking.	You aren't walking.
He / She / It is walking.	He / She / It is not walking.	He / She / It isn't walking.
We are walking.	We are not walking.	We aren't walking.
You are walking.	You are not walking.	You aren't walking.
They are walking.	They are not walking.	They aren't walking.

Forma interrogativa	Risposte brevi – Affermative	Risposte brevi – Negative
Am I walking?	Yes, you are.	No, you aren't.
Are you walking?	Yes, I am.	No, I'm not.
Is he / she / it walking?	Yes, he / she / it is.	No, he / she / it isn't.
Are we walking?	Yes, we are.	No, we aren't.
Are you walking?	Yes, you are.	No, you aren't.
Are they walking?	Yes, they are.	No, they aren't.

Spelling variations

Regole ortografiche per la formazione della terza persona singolare del *Present simple*.

-ch, -sh, -ss, -x, -zz, -o	watch	wash	kiss	relax	buzz	do
-es	watch**es**	wash**es**	kiss**es**	relax**es**	buzz**es**	do**es**

consonante + *-y*	study	vocale + *-y*	play
-ies	stud**ies**	*-s*	play**s**

Regole ortografiche per la forma in *-ing*.

Forma base	eat	pla**y**	stud**y**	hav**e**	sto**p**	**lie**
Forma in *-ing*	eat**ing**	play**ing**	study**ing**	hav**ing**	stop**ping**	**lying**

Past simple

Forma affermativa	Forma negativa – Estesa	Forma negativa – Contratta
I walked.	I did not walk.	I didn't walk.
You walked.	You did not walk.	You didn't walk.
He / She / It walked.	He / She / It did not walk.	He / She / It didn't walk.
We walked.	We did not walk.	We didn't walk.
You walked.	You did not walk.	You didn't walk.
They walked.	They did not walk.	They didn't walk.

Forma interrogativa	Risposte brevi – Affermative	Risposte brevi – Negative
Did I walk?	Yes, you did.	No, you didn't.
Did you walk?	Yes, I did.	No, I didn't.
Did he / she / it walk?	Yes, he / she / it did.	No, he / she / it didn't.
Did we walk?	Yes, we did.	No, we didn't.
Did you walk?	Yes, you did.	No, you didn't.
Did they walk?	Yes, they did.	No, they didn't.

Present perfect

Forma affermativa		Forma negativa	
Estesa	Contratta	Estesa	Contratta
I have walked.	I've walked.	I have not walked.	I haven't walked.
You have walked.	You've walked.	You have not walked.	You haven't walked.
He / She / It has walked.	He's / She's / It's walked.	He / She / It has not walked.	He / She / It hasn't walked.
We have walked.	We've walked.	We have not walked.	We haven't walked.
You have walked.	You've walked.	You have not walked.	You haven't walked.
They have walked.	They've walked.	They have not walked.	They haven't walked.

Forma interrogativa	Risposte brevi – Affermative	Risposte brevi – Negative
Have I walked?	Yes, you have.	No, you haven't.
Have you walked?	Yes, I have.	No, I haven't.
Has he / she / it walked?	Yes, he / she / it has.	No, he / she / it hasn't.
Have we walked?	Yes, we have.	No, we haven't.
Have you walked?	Yes, you have.	No, you haven't.
Have they walked?	Yes, they have.	No, they haven't.

be going to

Forma affermativa		Forma negativa	
Estesa	Contratta	Estesa	Contratta
I am going to walk.	I'm going to walk.	I am not going to walk.	I'm not going to walk.
You are going to walk.	You're going to walk.	You are not going to walk.	You aren't going to walk.
He / She / It is going to walk.	He / She / It's going to walk.	He / She / It is not going to walk.	He / She / It isn't going to walk.
We are going to walk.	We're going to walk.	We are not going to walk.	We aren't going to walk.
You are going to walk.	You're going to walk.	You are not going to walk.	You aren't going to walk.
They are going to walk.	They're going to walk.	They are not going to walk.	They aren't going to walk.

Forma interrogativa	Risposte brevi – Affermative	Risposte brevi – Negative
Am I going to walk...?	Yes, you are.	No, you aren't.
Are you going to walk...?	Yes, I am.	No, I'm not.
Is he / she / it going to walk...?	Yes, he / she / it is.	No, he / she / it isn't.
Are we going to walk... ?	Yes, we are.	No, we aren't.
Are you going to walk... ?	Yes, you are.	No, you aren't.
Are they going to walk... ?	Yes, they are.	No, they aren't.

Base form	Past simple	Past participle	In italiano
be	was, were	been	*essere*
become	became	become	*diventare*
begin	began	begun	*iniziare*
break	broke	broken	*rompere*
bring	brought	brought	*portare*
build	built	built	*costruire*
buy	bought	bought	*comprare*
catch	caught	caught	*prendere, afferrare*
choose	chose	chosen	*scegliere*
come	came	come	*venire*
cost	cost	cost	*costare*
cut	cut	cut	*tagliare*
do	did	done	*fare*
draw	drew	drawn	*disegnare*
dream	dreamed / dreamt	dreamed / dreamt	*sognare*
drive	drove	driven	*guidare*
drink	drank	drunk	*bere*
eat	ate	eaten	*mangiare*
fall	fell	fallen	*cadere*
feel	felt	felt	*sentire, provare*
fight	fought	fought	*combattere, litigare*
find	found	found	*trovare*
fly	flew	flown	*volare*
forget	forgot	forgotten	*dimenticare*
forgive	forgave	forgiven	*perdonare*
get	got	got / gotten	*ricevere, ottenere*
give	gave	given	*dare*
go	went	gone	*andare*
grow	grew	grown	*crescere*
have	had	had	*avere*
hear	heard	heard	*sentire, udire*
hit	hit	hit	*colpire*
keep	kept	kept	*tenere, mantenere*
know	knew	known	*sapere, conoscere*
learn	learned / learnt	learned / learnt	*imparare*
leave	left	left	*lasciare, partire*
lend	lent	lent	*prestare*
let	let	let	*permettere, lasciare*
lose	lost	lost	*perdere*
make	made	made	*fare, fabbricare*
mean	meant	meant	*significare, intendere*
meet	met	met	*incontrare, conoscere*
pay	paid	paid	*pagare*
put	put	put	*mettere*
read /ri:d/	read /red/	read /red/	*leggere*
ride	rode	ridden	*cavalcare*

Base form	Past simple	Past participle	In italiano
ring	rang	rung	*suonare, squillare*
run	ran	run	*correre*
say	said	said	*dire*
see	saw	seen	*vedere*
sell	sold	sold	*vendere*
send	sent	sent	*spedire, mandare*
show	showed	showed / shown	*mostrare*
shut	shut	shut	*chiudere*
sing	sang	sung	*cantare*
sit	sat	sat	*sedere*
sleep	slept	slept	*dormire*
speak	spoke	spoken	*parlare*
spend	spent	spent	*spendere, passare, trascorrere*
stand	stood	stood	*stare (in piedi)*
swim	swam	swum	*nuotare*
take	took	taken	*prendere*
teach	taught	taught	*insegnare*
tell	told	told	*dire, raccontare*
think	thought	thought	*pensare*
throw	threw	thrown	*gettare, buttare*
understand	understood	understood	*capire*
wake	woke	woken	*svegliarsi*
wear	wore	worn	*indossare*
win	won	won	*vincere*
write	wrote	written	*scrivere*

Notes

Notes